This book invites the soul to a ⟨...⟩ ⟨...⟩f
grace and it offers a vision of h⟨...⟩ ⟨...⟩o
age is more in need of the ra⟨...⟩ ⟨...⟩d
daughters of God. We strive en⟨...⟩ ⟨...⟩re exhausted, de-
pleted, and lonely. Is this the abundant life? What is the problem? Few have the courage of Rose Marie Miller to say it
simply and forthrightly—the problem is self-righteousness.
Rose Marie offers us a profoundly personal and painful
glimpse into her story, exposes the dark corners of our self-
righteousness, and invites us to dance with God. Get ready to
party.
—**Dan Allender,** psychologist, speaker, and author of *Bold
Love* and *The Wounded Heart*

God is using Jack and Rose Marie Miller's work and Sonship
seminars to do a deep work in many people's lives. No ministry today more effectively communicates the love of Christ to
the hearts of people.
—**Larry Crabb**, psychologist, author, and speaker

This book gave me a new perspective and a clearer vision of
how God's grace frees and steadies his children. I would rec-
ommend it to anyone who has been burdened by guilt, anger,
or anxiety and yet has believed in Christ.
—**Valerie Shephard**, pastor's wife and mother of eight

Rose Marie Miller's story is simple, fresh, and engaging.
There is something in her self-disclosure that opens small permanent fissures in my own heart. The Word is able to seep
into these cracks, renewing me in God's grace and enacting
desperately needed changes.
—**John Smed,** Coordinator of Church Planting, Mission to
North America, Presbyterian Church of America

Mrs. Miller's story has touched me deeply, offering hope that
God could touch others' lives through me with the power of
Jesus' love, not by my own efforts. Once you begin this journey through ten key years of Rose Marie's life, you won't
want to stop—it's a real page-turner. And watch out—God's
grace might transform you too.
—**Connie McDowell,** businesswoman and pastor's wife

In this book and in their teaching about Sonship, Jack and Rose Marie Miller are developing and applying the most authentic aspect of Calvin's theology concerning the Christian life: union with Christ as adopted sons and daughters.
—**Douglas Kelly,** Professor of Systematic Theology at Reformed Theological Seminary

This is a beautiful book, worth writing and very much worth reading. You have given a lot just to your children and grandchildren by leaving this record of grace working in your life. I hope many others will also read it.
—**Barbara Juliani,** Rose Marie's daughter and coauthor of *Come Back, Barbara*

This book is written with the intent to disturb you so much that you get spiritually renewed by Jesus. It is one of the few books today that deserves to be read and reread and reread.
—**David McCarty,** U.S. Director, World Harvest Mission

As I taught this book to women who lived in the inner city, Rose Marie's struggle to see herself as loved because of Christ's righteousness, and not because of her own achievements, mirrored their own struggle to find grace, and to know Christ's presence in the face of disappointing results.
—**Mrs. Ruth Correnti,** inner city pastor's wife

In a world where it is tempting to try to explain and manage everything, Rose Marie confronts us with the truth that there are no guarantees in life. When our dreams are frustrated, we can either try to manage on our own by withdrawing, getting busy, or becoming bitter or overwhelmed, or we can return to Jesus, putting our hope in his Word, believing his promises, and finding comfort.
—**Joanne Stahl,** Sonship Discipler and Consultant, World Harvest Mission

FROM
FEAR
TO
freedom

LIVING AS SONS &
DAUGHTERS OF GOD

ROSE MARIE MILLER

Harold Shaw Publishers
Wheaton, Illinois

ISBN 0-87788-259-2

Cover design by David LaPlaca

Library of Congress Cataloging in-Publication Data

Miller, Rose Marie, 1924-
    From fear to freedom : living as sons and daughters of God /
Rose Marie Miller.
        p. cm.
    ISBN 0-87788-259-2 (pbk.)
    1. Miller, Rose Marie, 1924- . 2. Presbyterians—United States—
Biography. 3. Justification. 4. Christian life—Presbyterian authors.
I. Title.
BX9225. M457A3 1994
285.1'092—dc20   94-13660

---

99 98 97 96 95 94

10 9 8 7 6 5 4 3 2

To Jack, my husband, friend, and partner,

who always saw more potential in me

than I saw in myself;

To my children and grandchildren

who are heirs to the legacy

of transforming grace;

And to the men and women who,

weary of acting like orphans,

have discovered again the delight

of being sons and daughters

of their Father in heaven;

I dedicate this book.

CONTENTS

Foreword

Rose Marie's testimony is that the reality of being sons and daughters of God is at the heart of the Christian life, and to miss it is to live like an orphan robbed of joy. She has the kind of excitement about Christ and the forgiving grace of the gospel that Francis Schaeffer had in his life when during a crisis he had newly discovered "the present value of the blood of Christ."

There is a hunger among people today to get to the heart of the New Testament message. Becky Morgan, a lawyer in Asheville, North Carolina, recently wrote to Rose Marie about how her sonship teaching is helping her and a good friend. She says, "About a year ago, a close friend of mine, wife of a local pastor, got your Sonship series, and radical changes began to occur. Though a seminary graduate, she said it was as if she'd never heard of justification by faith!" Becky explains:

> She and I had been praying together for revival . . . . We'd been brought to repentance over some deep sins in our families and over pride in ministry. We'd been devouring everything we could get by Dr. Lloyd-Jones and biographies of Whitefield, Edwards, and Spurgeon, . . . trying to get "ruthlessly honest" before Christ. And then came your training series—and the message of sonship and grace has come into sharp focus. We are so excited. Another friend, a leader in ministry to women, struggling with a perfectionistic "fix-it" kind of personal history, has been profoundly impacted—especially by your testimony, Rose Marie.

Becky and her friends are saying that they, like Rose Marie, have been surprised by grace and that they keep being surprised by grace. They marvel at the liberation that comes when you no longer think of the gospel as a message relevant only to non-Christians.

When Rose Marie begins her book, she is frustrated with me, and I am frustrated with her. Who can break the relational logjam? Neither of us. But once the gospel had gripped me deeply in the center of my own conscious life, I was able to pursue a whole new relationship with her.

My first attempts to love her more deeply were halting and often stumbling. I still concealed a judgmental attitude beneath a veneer of niceness. But I did get hold of one anchor truth: The awesome self-sacrifice of Christ means that God is for me. I have been incredibly affirmed by my Father; and in turn my calling as a son is to affirm others—not to condemn them.

So I began to affirm Rose Marie. I worked out a principle: I should affirm or praise her ninety-nine times before I criticized her once. Of course, I never did any of this perfectly, but my more frequent affirmations gave her a new security in our relationship. It enabled us to begin a slow move from defensive avoidance of painful differences, marred by occasional destructive conflicts, into a period of constructive conflict.

This new openness cost us both much pain. Rose Marie's candor in criticizing me gave the resident Pharisee a dose of his own medicine. My new freely expressed appreciation for Rose Marie also cleared the way for her to inquire into the roots of faith for herself—and, to quote her, "to see how I was using the role of victim to keep Jack at a distance and God out of my life."

She knows all about my wobblings, and has treated me with all kindness in this book. I also know about her sometimes falling back into an orphan mindset. Now and then we still have conflicts. But we have together discovered something deeply practical about grace as we pray together. We have more than the words about grace; we have begun to hear the music. As one sings the song of the gospel, the music sets you free and you know how to set other people free from fear and guilt.

Rose Marie invites you to listen to her song about grace and then join in. Here is the music: "It is for freedom that Christ has set us free" (Gal. 5:1).

By now you have guessed it. I love Rose Marie and I love her song.

C. John "Jack" Miller

Acknowledgments

I wish to thank my husband, Jack, for his valuable teaching and insistence that I put in permanent form the truth of the gospel of grace as it impacted my life. My grateful thanks to my children, who continued to honor me through the difficult years this book describes. My intellectual debt to Florence Allshorn, Richard Lovelace, Ray Stedman, C. S. Lewis, and R. C. Sproul is greater than I can express. My thanks to Sue Lutz, who believed enough in what I wrote to do the major editing necessary to make the book readable. A special thanks to Laura Keyser for all her work in getting this book ready for the publisher. I am grateful to the many men and women who read the manuscript, whose lives were deeply impacted and said, "This book must be published." They are too numerous to mention, but they know who they are.

Acknowledgments

Introduction:
My Life As a Window

It takes a certain amount of courage to write a book as personal as this one. At least it required courage from me, as I relived difficult experiences and sought to distill what they had taught me for the pages of this book.

It also takes a certain amount of confidence that what you have to share has value and relevance for others. Such confidence, when God-given, expresses faith that God has something for you to share. Otherwise it is mere presumption. I have kept at it because I believe that my life really is a window through which you can observe God's grace at work.

This is a book about sonship and the freedom of the sons and daughters of God. It is a call to liberation for women, and men too, who labor under a burden of unfulfilled longing, anxiety, and plain old-fashioned guilt—and who have not yet given up the idea of salvation through trying harder and self-effort.

This book celebrates grace. Life in its essence is like an encroaching rim of fire which entraps, a peril often coming from our own discontents. The paradox is that grace comes only to the helpless, those who know they are trapped and yet have found the courage to admit that they can find no answer to their problem in themselves or others. They have escaped hopelessness by asking for grace.

This is the story of the ten most turbulent years of my life and yet, in a mysterious way, the best ones. At the time I felt more a sense of pain than an awareness of liberation. If you had told me I was learning about freedom, liberation, and joy, I would have laughed or maybe cried. For during these years I stumbled and struggled through six difficult and painful crises:

- My husband's decision to be a pastor
- The unexpected rebellion of my daughter
- A midlife marital crisis
- My realization that I could not love people
- The discovery of the power of generational sins inherited from my parents
- My struggle with and inability to understand submission

For most of my life, I had too much strength of a sort—strength to help others and to mislead myself about the nature of grace. In my blindness and ignorance I developed coping strategies. For example, I love order; it seems to promise so much. I believed that if I had outward order, then my heart would be at peace. This strategy worked until my first crisis, when I discovered that I could not control myself or my circumstances. Then, when my life was no longer under control, another need surfaced—a strange, haunting longing for something free and fresh. I wanted freedom. Especially freedom from the guilt that stormed into my life when I became embittered with the people who had destabilized my world.

Betty Friedan wrote in her immensely influential book *The Feminine Mystique* that the modern woman is troubled by "an unnamed problem." Friedan says that there is about today's woman a haunting discontent and a longing for fulfillment. She names "others" as the cause of modern woman's basic problem and claims that freedom is realized by liberation from these others—especially dominating males. In her view, once woman is free from male dominance she can take control of her own life.

When my story begins I had not yet read Betty Friedan's book. But there was a lot in me that instinctively said yes to her idea that my problem was other people and their dominance. I had a longing for freedom and was absolutely convinced that others were the cause of my bondage.

Liv Ullman, however, points out something I learned in my own attempts to find freedom. In her book *Choices*, Ullman calls it "the dilemma of the liberated woman." She says of her decision to pursue her own autonomy:

> But after choice [autonomous freedom] there was a new set of rules, not necessarily tied to women's liberation, because after liberation from authority followed pressure: all the new ideas crashing in on women who were not sure how to direct their new found independence. The liberated woman followed in the stream of others who, equally liberated, said what everybody else was saying, read what everybody else was reading, conformed to that which everybody else conformed to.[1]

Betty Friedan named the hunger for us, and gave her solution. But Liv Ullman describes the frustrating consequences. You become free *from* what and *for* what? For pressure? For a new set of rules laid down by dominating women who say they are liberated from dominating men? No, modern woman started out wanting to be free from pressure, and that freedom is what she must have. But it cannot come from inventing herself all over again. No one of us has that power. We are not God, and only God can make or remake a person.

My sense is that most women today often unconsciously long for the kind of life that God wishes to give them. Many Christian women today are not in sympathy with liberationist movements, but they have the same heart hunger for freedom. They just do not know how to obtain it.

In order for me to find freedom and continue to live it out in my life, God needed to name my unnamed problem. His definition was, "Rose Marie, you have the mindset of an orphan." This is how the orphan mental attitude works:

- Life consciously or unconsciously is centered on personal autonomy and moral will power, with grace understood as God's maintaining your own strength—not as his transforming power.

- Faith is defined as trying harder to do and be better, with a view to establishing a good record leading to self-justification.

- Obedience is related to external, visible duties, with attitudes and deeper motivation virtually ignored.

- "What people think" is represented as the real moral standard, based upon visible success and failure.

- An *I-am-a-victim* attitude is supported by coping strategies, wall building, blame shifting, gossiping, and defending.

- All this is accompanied by *intense* feelings of aloneness, believing that no one understands and that one is trapped by circumstances.

In the summer of 1973 my husband, Jack, was lecturing on grace in the carriage house in the back of our yard:

Two seventeenth-century theologians were debating on the nature of grace. One said that grace is like one parent guiding a toddler across the room to the other parent, who has an apple for the child. The nearby parent watches the youngster; if he almost falls, this parent will hold him for a moment so that he can still cross the room under his own power. But the other theologian had a different view. For him grace comes to us only in the discovery of our total helplessness. In his concept,

> we are like a caterpillar in a ring of fire. Deliverance can only come from above.

When I first heard this, my heart agreed, *Yes, that is me. I'm trapped by a ring of fire, and I don't see any way of escape or help.* At the time I was more impressed by the image of encroaching fire than by the rescue from above.

Later I came to delight in the idea that grace is the Father's hand reaching down to pull Rose Marie out of the circle of fire. Today my heart says, *That's me. I'm trapped and I see that I cannot escape.* But now I add, *But Jesus will reach down from above when I cry out for help. He will rescue me.*

Here then is my theme: the only hope of liberation for a helpless, resisting caterpillar in a ring of fire is deliverance from above. Someone must reach down into the ring and take us out. This rescue is what brings us from the orphan state into that of the son or daughter. This is not mere supporting grace, but transforming grace.

I present no formulas. I want you to learn to think more clearly about your own rings of fire and God as the omnipotent Rescuer. Grace is received through the plea of the desperate. You have taken the sinner's place, and you now discover that a hand from above mysteriously rescues you. The first discovery of this transforming grace establishes God as your Father. You are permanently in his family. Still, you renew your relationship with the Father again and again by seeking the same transforming grace which first brought you into sonship or daughtership.

Explore with me the dimensions of grace that set me free to live as a daughter. It is my sincere hope that this story will not so much help you to know me, but to know God and to see yourself through his eyes.

Here is the window; open your eyes and look.

---

1. Liv Ullman, *Choices* (New York: Alfred A. Knopf, 1984), p. 7.

Part I

THE SPIRITUAL ORPHAN

I will not leave you as orphans. I will come to you.

Jesus (John 14:18)

1

Awakening to Failure: A Midlife Crisis

The very first tear he made was so deep that I thought it had gone right into my heart. And when [Aslan] began to tear the skin off, it hurt worse than anything I've ever felt.—C. S. Lewis, *The Voyage of the Dawn Treader*

They say it's always darkest just before dawn. I wonder if there is a parallel proverb that says it's always brightest before the darkest night. In 1971, my life had reached its brightest point in many ways. Yet just a few turns in the road left me in the darkness of pain and deep confusion.

But first the sunlight. That year it seemed to pour in through the windows and doors of our family's big, old, inviting home in Jenkintown, Pennsylvania, a Philadelphia suburb. Over the years, what has been distinctive about our rambling house has not been the furnishings as much as the people who have made their way through it. In 1971, our front and back doors welcomed a group of the most unique and intriguing people that have graced our lives before or since.

Jack and I had been married for twenty-one years. He was teaching in a theological seminary and pastoring a church twenty miles away in a small village called Mechanicsville. I was busy at home, raising our four unmarried children (our eldest, Roseann, had just been married) and caring for my elderly mother and my retarded sister, Barbara, who lived with us. It was an exciting—even exhilarating—time for both of us.

The church Jack pastored was attracting many unchurched people. They ranged from upper-middle-class businessmen to many troubled youth. Though we lived some distance from the church, the hope of Jack's gospel message and his love for them led many of these folk to our door. That summer, our house overflowed with people who wanted to talk with Jack about a Christ they had never seriously considered before. Jack and I, along with our children, worked hard to make our home a house of refuge for many hurting people.

Jack had recently undergone a spiritual revival of his own. His newfound joy and excitement about the gospel made people want to learn more. Jack spent many hours explaining why God's promise of grace offers so much hope, and how the blood of Jesus, shed on the cross, is powerful enough to change anyone.

This was of considerable interest, especially to the young people. Some of them had been in prison, others in mental institutions. Some had experimented with the occult and drugs. Others were girls who had run with motorcycle gangs. Their skepticism gave way to the first stirrings of hope that the gospel could actually apply to them in their situations. Jack told them, "Repent of your sins and trust in Christ's death and resurrection, and you will have a completely new life." Many of them believed, and found that it was so.

But as you might guess, some of them needed help restructuring their lives as new Christians. Both Jack and I had a desire to help them in this, and we laid this burden before our four children living at home. Ruth was studying at nearby Beaver College. Our son Paul was in his first year at Temple University. Our daughters Barbara and Keren were in the Jenkintown public schools; Barbara, a high-school junior, and Keren, a fifth grader. They agreed to share our home with hurting people, and a grand and tumultuous adventure in hospitality began.

A Lifestyle of Ministry

One of our most memorable guests that summer was Ann, the sixteen-year-old daughter of friends. Ann came to us from a state mental hospital. There her violent anger had erupted during a therapy session and she had attacked her psychiatrist, hitting her so hard that her jaw was sore for three weeks. The hospital staff had insisted that Ann needed a modified lobotomy to stay, but Ann's distraught parents found that hard to accept. So did we, and despite warnings that Ann was violent and dangerous, she became a member of our family in June.

Ann proved to be cooperative in our home. She had some problems with physical coordination, a fact that triggered her impatience and anger. Fortunately, life with my sister Barbara helped me to understand Ann's frustration, as did a previous job as a teacher's aide in a school for children with learning and emotional disabilities. I knew the importance of giving them careful and systematic training in basic physical skills. And that kind of training was something I especially enjoyed doing.

I worked with Ann until she learned to set the table and do the dishes without too much disarray. We went over the laying out of plates and silverware again and again until she could do it better. I made her our home's official greeter, and soon she was doing an exceptional job cheerfully welcoming our visitors.

Jack concentrated more on the internal struggles. He began to teach Ann about finding hope and confidence in God. She instinctively wanted to talk to him about her behavior. Her first words in the morning usually were, "Do you think I'll ever get to the bottom of my problems?"

Typically, Jack would smile and say, "Ann, we are there already. It's just that you are a sinner like me. But God loves sinners." His upbeat summary usually allayed Ann's fears and eased her into the day.

It was not all roses. One day while Jack was out, Ann's famous temper began to erupt. But I refused to be intimidated by Ann, and she knew it. We talked things out, and our near-conflict ended peaceably. After six weeks, Ann regularly greeted visitors, set the table for our many guests, and helped Jack with the yard work. Soon she was going home on weekends.

We had other guests, too. Again, my role centered on how faith worked itself out in the externals of life, while Jack did more of the inner probing. We sought to help our new friends learn to work and help one another. Showing courtesy, eating meals together, working around the house, and going to church—these were the four simple rules we expected everyone to follow. We let no one act like an idle house guest. We were family, and in our family everyone laughed and worked together.

Too often, stories of this kind of all-absorbing ministry carry the sad postscript that the children of the ministry couple stand on the sidelines, suffering neglect. I know with certainty that we did not handle everything properly during this time, but our children's involvement in these needy lives gave us the unexpected blessing of seeing spiritual growth in their hearts too. Jack's emphasis that "I am a sinner, you are a sinner, and God's grace is for sinners" wound up working in their lives as well. To me, this was the ultimate confirmation that God was pleased with what we were doing.

We noticed it first in our eldest daughter, Roseann, who had come home for the summer while her husband Jim went through basic training at Fort Dix, New Jersey. Roseann watched and listened to her father as he sat by the hour talking to people about Christ. One day she came to us and said, "I saw all these people change, and I knew that I needed deep changes in me. I went to the bedroom, got down on my knees, confessed every sin I could think of, and came out a new woman."

Another day, blonde, blue-eyed Jill drove to the house with a popular young man from the local high school who wanted to talk to Jack. She sat out in the car waiting for him, but finally came in, impatient with whatever was taking him so long. She sat in our living room and listened intently as Jack explained the gospel to her friend. After twenty minutes, she burst into tears and said, "I want that. I want to become a Christian." She became a Christian that day. Not long after that, she dropped her boyfriend. And not long after that, she became engaged to our son Paul!

The Best of Everything
These were wonderful days for me. I was watching God change the most hopeless of people, and now I was seeing

him change our family and provide Christian spouses for Roseann and Paul. Our children had taken their stand as active and dedicated Christians. Our daughter Barbara was spending the summer working at the London L'Abri, a Christian ministry to intellectuals and displaced persons, led by Dick and Mardi Keyes.

And there was more. Sometime that summer, a talented young musician and seminary student named Jim Correnti came to dinner to learn about pastoring and theology from Jack. Over our evening meal he met our daughter Ruth, and after that we saw a great deal more of him. Ruth's life was also changing in a fundamental way, and before the summer was over, she and Jim were engaged to be married. As a mother, my cup was filled to overflowing.

The wedding date was set for the Friday after Thanksgiving. With much gratitude to God, and perhaps some self-congratulation, I watched Ruth walk down the aisle on her father's arm. The building was overflowing with people. Downstairs in the church fellowship hall, long tables covered in white were laden with cakes, breads, candies, and a beautiful three-tiered wedding cake.

My eyes filled with tears as I listened to the bridal couple take their vows. My heart filled with bright images of all the good things that had happened to our family. I remembered Roseann's wedding just nine months before in our little country church. She had walked down the aisle on the arm of her grandfather, my dad. That image was especially poignant to me as he died just six weeks later. In the intervening months, I had seen the outpouring of spiritual blessing and power that I have just described.

As I heard Jack tell Jim, "You may kiss the bride," I thought to myself, *Life couldn't be better. All my children are Christians. I can be confident of their future.* To me it made sense. This was the goal I had been working toward all my life. Didn't I have faith? Wasn't the universe founded on a moral order, and tilted in favor of the hard-working and the righteous? Hadn't Jack and I been faithful in training our children in the things of God? We had worked hard to teach them the

Bible, to memorize the catechism, to give them a Christian school education. We taught them to honor us as parents, to acquire good manners, to be responsible, and to work hard. Now I was seeing the fruit of my labor.

Collapse of Illusions

As it turned out, the fruit of my labor contained the seeds of its own destruction, though I did not realize it at the time. Ruth's wedding was in many ways a climactic affirmation of the life I had sought to live before God and other people. But it became an event that devastated my view of myself and all I had done with my life.

It started innocently enough one afternoon when a friend and I were having tea together in our sun-filled living room. She commented casually, "Jim and Ruth's wedding was lovely, Rose Marie, but it's too bad that you ran out of food before the wedding party was served."

I was stunned. My mental world darkened. All the beautiful memories of Ruth's wedding faded under the exposure of a social failure. I thought, *I have let down Jim's family, Jim, Ruth, and our many friends.* I couldn't shake the intense feelings of shame and guilt. For months I was fixated on my failure as a mother at Ruth's wedding.

Friends had offered to provide extra food and drink for the wedding, but confident of my own planning, I had declined their offers with thanks. Now, instead of facing up to this obvious character flaw in myself—my presumptuous self-confidence—I concluded that God had let me down when I needed him.

Unleashed Guilt

It doesn't surprise me now that this coping device—ignoring my own sins and failures and blaming God instead—didn't work. Instead, it only deepened my burden of shame and my preoccupation with the incident. And it also roused other feelings of guilt out of their state of hibernation, feelings that I had unconsciously suppressed. These feelings related to my dear father. These were even deeper shadows and darker valleys that I could not leave behind.

My dad had been a very special person to me, and a very important part of the family order as I grew up. He was most predictable and amazingly faithful in performing his duties in the family—traits that I valued highly for the security they gave me. In 1965, he moved from California with Mother and my sister Barbara to the apartment in the second floor of our home.

The morning he died, in March 1971, my sister had come to tell me that Dad was sick. I was getting ready to take a shower. As soon as I was through, I went up to the second floor. I found Dad on the bed—dead from a massive brain hemorrhage.

My sense of shame was very strong. I had not done my duty for Dad at the time of his death. I should have gone right upstairs to find out how sick he really was. Unease over my guilty failure was persistent and real. I had betrayed my father, my lifetime friend, violating the family order at its most fundamental level. And yet, even at the time of his death, I never talked these feelings through with Jack. I chose not to think about my sorrow, and I suppressed my feelings. I thought that I was strong enough to handle my loss and guilt. For a time I was, but my failure at Ruth's wedding unleashed these old feelings of unresolved guilt.

As this sense of shame came crashing down on me, even I could see that I was having some kind of emotional crisis—a midlife passage. But I did not see that this crisis had its roots in a deeper faith problem. I did not realize that the confidence I had always had about my life was not faith, as I had assumed, but a reliance on my own competency, be it real or imagined. When my competency was called into question by my failures in life's momentous events, like my father's death and my daughter's wedding, my confidence—and the world it supported—began to crumble. And yet, because I thought I was living by faith, I did not understand what was happening.

Presumptive self-confidence may look like faith, but it has a very different spiritual root (Jer. 17:5-10). Faith and presumption look alike because both qualities are characterized by confidence, but faith begins in the recognition and acceptance of our total human weakness. It relies solely on God and his gracious willingness to empower us.

Presumption, on the other hand, is a reliance on human moral abilities and religious accomplishments, on visible securities. It ultimately relies on human will power to serve God and people. In my case, I was unknowingly relying on Jack, or past successes, or my own abilities. And I came to see that a mix of presumption and faith produces a personal instability that surfaces in crises and major life transitions.

Presumption is a reliance on human moral abilities and religious accomplishments, on visible securities.

From God's point of view, the lack of faith is a great evil, the root of countless other evils. In James 1, we learn that in times of deeper testing, many religious people appear "wave-driven" and "double-minded." Such people cannot "receive anything from the Lord" (James 1:6-7). Faith alone links life to God and his abundant, fatherly grace. If this communication line is cut, the soul wanders alone, orphanlike.

This has never been an easy thing to see, but the difficulty is heightened today by our determination to reduce every problem and sin to its psychological manifestations. I was also confused because I did have some measure of true faith, but it was tainted—and rendered powerless—by my presumptive trust in my own strength.

How God Reaches Us

How does God deal with such a hidden sin pattern in his children? First he must expose it. What does presumptive faith depend on for its existence? It must have positive circumstances and feelings of success based on visible accomplishments. So when God wants to reach us, he must take away those favorable circumstances and accomplishments.

He hits hard at our false trusts. Our confidence in ourselves is shaken by life changes; we fight back. We increase our demands upon our "strengths," be they inner qualities, outer achievements, or other people. But only emptiness follows. Like the orphan we cry, "I am abandoned," when in fact God's grace is pursuing us ever more intensely.

Today I can see the love behind the Father's plan. But back then I thought my fundamental problems were psychological, emotional, and marital. Today I can see that the root of my problem was that I did not know God personally with any depth. I did not even know what was going on in my own rebellious heart. I was actively resisting grace and its implications for the way I lived my life, but I did not know it.

So God left me alone, so to speak, that the revelation of my insufficiency would also show me God's sufficiency. He was withdrawing his presence so that I would reach out to his grace for help. He was saying to me, his demanding creature, "I have let you bring yourself to this place of loneliness and guilt. Now I want you to listen to me."

I wish I could say I listened. I didn't. I read a lot of Christian how-to books to cope with my problems, but they failed me, because I filtered them through the grid of my self-trust and self-reliance. I really thought that method and technique and new kinds of order and organization were the level at which my problems could be solved.

"I Don't Get Any Help"

I remember standing outside the church one evening after a service. A few of us were talking about the parable of the friend asking for help at midnight (Luke 11:5-13). Jack related the story to our calling as God's sons and daughters. "As children of the heavenly Father," he said, "our biggest need is to constantly ask the Father for the bread of the Holy Spirit."

For just a moment, a match of hope flared in the darkness of my weary guilt and blind presumption. I was inclined to ask more questions, but the orphan in me said no. I drew back instead into the growing self-pity that comes so easily to a person trying to live without grace. I remember thinking, as I was in the midst of that busy year of ministry, *I help everyone else, but I don't seem to get any help in return.*

To my shame, I suppressed the promptings of the Holy Spirit that night. I could have turned to him for conviction and teaching about the nature of faith and grace and what it means to be a child of God, but instead I turned destructively inward.

I remember thinking, as I was in the midst of that busy year of ministry, I help everyone else, but I don't seem to get any help in return.

In so doing, I injured my emotional life. I had not opened up. Instead, I closed up more tightly. Healing can only come when this process is reversed. And there was something else I needed to see even more: My refusal to heed the Holy Spirit was the evil of unbelief (Heb. 3:12-13).

Soon my spirit was reaping the consequences. I discovered that I did not have the power to stop the growing self-condemnation taking over my thought life. Self-condemnation plagued me, yet I was not even willing to admit to anyone else that I had a problem. A refusal to live in the power of the grace of God isolates a person from him, and from everyone else as well. Spiritually and emotionally, you truly do feel like an orphan.

Spiritual orphans see themselves as humble sufferers in their emotional pain. But in fact they are simply closed off people who are too proud and fearful (the two are closely related) to admit failure, imperfections, and sins, and acknowledge their complete dependence on God.

I was left alone with failures dominating my heart. *I cannot admit the shame of my failures,* I told myself. *Who could do that?*

Grace Glimpses

God often uses the deeply unsettling circumstances of life to reveal the presumptive self-trust that prevails in the life of a spiritual orphan.

> • You can detect this attitude in yourself by your response to life when it goes out of control. If you handle pain and suffering by blaming others, refusing to learn from God, and becoming defensive or angry, you have the self-trust of an orphan, not the faith of a son or daughter.

Prayer: Lord, make me willing to accept the pain of healthy self-examination. Show me the difference between the faith of a son or daughter and the presumptive self-trust of an orphan. Amen.

2

Facing the Pain: "I Don't Even Know If God Exists"

Faith helps us when we are down, but unbelief throws us down when we are up. . . . By faith we have our life in Christ's fullness, but by unbelief we starve and pine away. —John Bunyan, *The Complete Works of Bunyan*

The year 1971 ended with my life still dominated by the destructive pattern of failure and shame. Outwardly, my life was characterized by activist ministry to needy people in my home. Inwardly, I felt needier than all of them, without a clue as to how to escape my self-imposed imprisonment in graceless Christianity. My sense of guilt, loneliness, and abandonment increased, but my sense of duty and self-reliance never allowed it to show in anything I was doing. My shoulders sagged more and more, but I never dropped my self-imposed burden.

The Nest Is Emptied
In my personal life I faced a season of continued losses. With both Roseann and Ruth married, our nest was beginning to empty. In the months ahead, Barbara was scheduled to leave for college and Paul and Jill would be married. In two years, we would go from five children living at home to only one—blonde and cheerful Keren.

Just losing Roseann and Ruth showed me how much I depended on our well-structured family order. In the midst of our busy parenting years, neither Jack nor I had realized that no human order is ever permanent or fully satisfying. It did not occur to us to prepare for the days when our children would leave. Our children and our ministry were much more the center of our married life than we realized.

I felt very alone because my children were such a pivotal part of my life. My feelings of abandonment grew stronger every day, but, true to form, I put my will power to work. I decided to try even harder as a Christian. I prayed and read the Bible more diligently, but it all seemed so dry. Edgy and tense, I longed for something more. Predictably, my frustration translated into more intense criticism of myself and greater demands on Jack.

> *I prayed and read the Bible more diligently, but it all seemed so dry.*

I noticed that Jack tended to use his busyness in ministry to justify his thoughtlessness toward me. "Your programs are more important to you than my needs and concerns," I complained. I don't think I had ever said anything like that to him before.

I expected Jack to jump and fill the void that my complaints had brought to his attention. But he was threatened by my growing demands and confused by my new moodiness. It became evident that we did not have the intimacy and communication skills to navigate through a time of crisis. We had no problem talking about our successes together, but we did not know how to open up about our inner struggles. Our communication lacked depth of honesty. Jack seemed almost frightened of his demanding wife.

About this time, Jack resigned from the pastorate to devote more time to his seminary teaching. This enabled him to help more at home with our extended family and guests. But word kept spreading about what he had to say. Spiritually hungry folks came from all over to talk to him. He was sometimes overwhelmed, and providing hospitality to these many visitors was no longer a privilege.

I was now shouldering a double burden—the work itself, and the heavier burden of my resentment. I felt I did not deserve this life of weakness and overextendedness. I decided, *People drain me. I like working with them, but their needs are endless, and so many who come are so negative! I have needs of my own right now. Who will meet them?*

Overwhelmed as I was on the inside, I did not understand why Jack didn't do more to protect me from people who seemed to think I was indestructible. Today I can see that they got the idea from *me*. I wasn't about to announce to the world that I was too weak to serve as hostess to different sets of visitors all day. Instead, I saw myself as the victim of negative circumstances. I felt helpless because I could not admit my weakness.

But Jack could see my weakness; he arranged for a much-needed trip to Cuernevaca, Mexico, for a month.

Paradise Found!—and Lost

Cuernevaca lies sixty miles south of Mexico City, situated on a high plateau. I loved it. It is a city characterized by warm sunshine, tropical flowers, and hospitable Mexican people. We found ourselves staying in a beautiful hotel converted into a retreat center. I enjoyed just looking at the white tiled pool, radiant in the sunlight. Tall green ferns and pink and white azalea bushes surrounded it. Paradise found! Here I could get rested and swim to my heart's content.

After two weeks in all that graciousness and beauty, Jack called home. Paul said, "Dad, Barb is running around with a crowd of people who are having a bad influence on her." Jack asked our daughter if she would like to visit us in Mexico, and she reluctantly agreed to come.

After a few days of being together, the three of us attended a wedding where, from our point of view, Barb's flirtations with a male guest were highly inappropriate. We attempted to correct her for her behavior, but we overdid the correction, especially me. Barb's response was to announce emphatically, "I need my freedom. I don't find that Christianity helps me. I have tried it all, and it doesn't work for me."

I was stunned, numb. Then I took the Bible and began to read to her the promises of God, ending with the passages about hell. She sat in stone cold silence. At this I began to cry, but I still kept on reading. Then I began to shout. This went on for two hours. I didn't even give Jack a chance to say much. I was filled with the twin furies of anger and fear. Like the hurricane whose strength diminishes when it hits the shore, I finally stopped. By then, everyone was exhausted.

I couldn't make sense of Barbara's behavior. The change seemed to have come overnight. I dislike surprises, especially those that upset family order, and suddenly I had a huge one on my hands! *To have one of my own children reject me and what I believe—it's as if God is rejecting me,* I thought.

I was left with a shredding of my whole soul. Forgotten was the warm sunshine. I could not see any beauty in the flowers. Within a few hours Cuernavaca had become paradise lost. I was only aware of incredible fear, a sharp pain in my chest, and a sinking feeling in the pit of my stomach.

It would have been so much better had I said, "Barbara, I am deeply ashamed of losing my temper. Will you forgive me?" My whole aim then should have been to make it clear that though I may have strongly disagreed with what she did, I would always, with unconditional love, accept her as my daughter.

The irony was that I had not undergone a thoroughgoing repentance in my own life, and here I was expecting it of my daughter. Perhaps the breach with Barbara would not have been so serious if, instead of going off the deep end, I had asked honest questions about her doubts and fears, especially since some of them were my own.

At first, Jack and I backed off from Barbara. But Jack recovered sooner than I and reached out to her. My world, including its Christian convictions, was shaken to its foundations.

When Barbara left for college that fall, the emotional and spiritual distance between us only widened.

The final blow came the next spring, in April 1973, when I opened a letter from Barbara that read, "Dear Mom and Dad, I know you won't like to hear this, but I am going to live with my boyfriend for the summer."

I felt as if I had been physically attacked. Although we asked many people to pray, I had little hope that it would do any immediate good. Barbara was so cold toward God and us. She was controlled by unbelief, and dominated by a mysterious blindness that I found utterly frightening.

By this time Jack was pastoring a brand-new church he had started, New Life Presbyterian Church in Jenkintown. Although it was less arduous than pastoring in Mechanicsville, the workload grew quickly. We again had people with very serious emotional and personal problems living in our home.

I supported Jack in the starting of the new church. But I also wanted Jack to take time to listen to my problems and feelings. My guilt and fears for Barbara were coupled with the bodily changes of menopause, and my feelings intensified. I demanded Jack's attention: "You pastor everyone else, and everyone else gets helped. Why don't you pastor me?" These verbal deluges rolled over him with such intensity that his own boat seemed in danger of swamping.

A Life-Changing Study

After almost a year of tension between us, Jack slowly began to change. At the time I did not know it, but the tensions in our relationship had driven him to the study of Galatians. Influenced by this study, he took his courage in his hands one evening, and asked me, "If there is one thing about me you would like to see changed, what would it be?"

Without the slightest hesitation, I said emphatically, "I would like you to listen."

Jack was taken completely by surprise. I can still remember the blank look on his face. No comprehension at all! Finally he asked, "Can you tell me why you say that?"

He listened as I talked about his shortcomings as a listening husband. I could see he was considering the matter as an entirely new thought. He did not say much. Not long afterwards he began an intensive study of the books of Leviticus, Deuteronomy, and Galatians. At first I did not see much change in him—at least none that I was ready to admit. But he was actually learning to listen to me. He also seemed to have lost his fears over Barbara.

In fact, he was soon seeing opportunities where I saw problems. The difference between us stood out as January 1974 approached, which was the date Barbara had set for her marriage to Tom, the young man with whom she had been living. Jack approached the event with cautious enthusiasm. He tried to make Tom his friend. He was open and relaxed with Barbara. I was impressed. Jack was also open with Barbara concerning his doubts over the marriage's survival. But having done that, he pitched in with freedom and graciousness and did everything in his power to help them. Barbara's friends gradually warmed to him.

After the wedding, Jack kept right on immersing himself in Galatians. He became less tense in his relationship with me, and began to affirm me in every way he could. Despite his efforts, my emotional demands intensified and my cumulative record of his wrongs grew longer. I thought, *He is a pastor and should know better.* I had assumed the outlook of so many people we had worked with. Many did not want to take responsibility for their lives and their destructive, self-centered behavior.

A Destructive Outlook

Like them, I told myself, "I am more sinned against than sinning." I had persuaded myself that my husband had wronged me, and it was going to take a lot of doing for him to get into my good graces again.

I look back now and marvel at how insensitive I was to my own blindness. Jack really did see how to help me, but I rebuffed his searching questions about the nature of faith and my understanding of Christ. He seemed to be wondering if I had confused faith with will power, and I was incensed by the suggestion! I had developed a perfect "orphan" mechanism for rejecting his care.

Here was the defensive pattern: One, I demanded help. Two, I defined the help as "someone to understand me." Three, I insisted that no one was trying to understand me. Four, I felt I deserved better than this. Five, I avoided taking responsibility for myself by often recalling "his failures." I had designed an impenetrable orphan circle. No one could get in and I could not get out, as I stubbornly rejected the very help I was demanding.

Add to this the fact that I was expecting from Jack what no human being could provide: the restoration of order to my emotional life, and truckloads of unconditional love. I wanted him to make me happy and to change everybody who came to talk to him—the sooner the better, so that they would not be a problem for me.

Somehow in my confusion God and Jack were identified in my mind as my control centers, and I hastily concluded that if Jack did not help me, God probably would not either. In my self-pity I especially wondered why God had stopped helping me. I had relied on God to bring order and security out of chaos, and yet here I was, trying hard to maintain order in my life, only to plunge deeper into guilt and inward isolation. I kept resolving to try harder to work out my "problems" but I could never seem to get to the bottom of them. I engaged in intense self-analysis, but this did nothing to alleviate my growing guilt and anxiety.

A Painful Confession

On our vacation to Tennessee that summer, we took Gail, a troubled young woman who was living with us. We drove down the Blue Ridge Parkway and camped in the Shenandoah National Park. That night, away from the active life that kept the most painful questions at bay, it took a long time for me to go to sleep. I lay in my sleeping bag and looked up at the stars, wondering, *Is there a personal Creator—a God who really cares?*

In Tennessee we stayed in the hospitable lakeside home of Fred and Leda. We planned to meet with Gail's parents there. The talks went well, but I had to tell Gail's parents the truth as I saw it, and that wasn't easy.

"Gail really isn't ready to be helped. She expects other people to help her, as if they had some kind of magic. She's pushed down so much anger and self-pity that she does not know who she is. We can't help her if she does not become an honest person. She's got to open up all the way."

Jack listened to me and shook his head as if he could not believe what he was hearing. "Excellent insight," Jack said later with a little smile playing on his face. Years afterward he told me with a chuckle, "Your description of Gail was almost a perfect self-description." I certainly couldn't have seen his point at the time. After all, no one could be more different from me than Gail! She could hardly get her act together to clean the bathroom. I was the one who upheld her and the whole household.

Is there a personal Creator— a God who really cares?

But after Gail went home with her parents, all the unexpressed hurts of the previous two years came to a head. As Jack and I strolled around the lake early one evening, I blurted out, "God seems like a dark cloud to me. I don't even know if he exists!"

My words came pouring out from the core of my being. For once I wasn't expecting Jack to do anything. For the first time in a very long time the real Rose Marie stood up, and I really didn't care if Jack responded with rejection or anger. I was just being completely honest.

I wasn't talking about this failure or that, or unfinished tasks, or people who wouldn't pull their weight at home. I was talking about intense, ghastly, dark loneliness, and uncontrolled surges of guilt and shame washing over me like endless waves on a deserted shore.

Jack didn't say anything. He simply accepted me in my struggle. He took me by the hand and we walked home, past the pines on the dirt road that led back to the house. He was shaken, but he placed no demand on me and offered no correction. The honesty had gone deep. The lights were gradually coming on for me.

The confusion and doubt I expressed that night had been hidden behind a life of outward performance. So many hurts, disappointments, and failures had been pressed down within me. It was as though I had a strong steel spring inside me which had been pushed down for years by habits of poor communication, by hurts in our marriage, by my outward conformity to the opinions of people, and by devotion to duty. But now the coils of steel were pushing up into my conscious mind issues long suppressed.

This was the first enlightenment of grace—the strong desire to be truthful about myself no matter what the cost. To stop making excuses and shifting blame. To open up to God and friends.

When we went home from vacation, Jack pulled from his shelf a copy of Martin Luther's commentary on Galatians, and photocopied the preface for me to read. "This," he said with a little smile, "will help you."

I was puzzled. I knew he had seen some amazing changes in people who had studied this material. But these people had all been highly perfectionistic folks, or irrational types or people controlled by obsessive sins. I didn't see what their experience had to do with me! They all seemed like hard-core rebels with massive demonologies. But my confession of doubt and despair had brought Jack to a new view of who I was. He finally admitted that *an outwardly righteous person like me might also be a hard-core rebel deep down.*

Reading Luther's writings only led to more questions. Somehow I knew that what Martin Luther wrote about the difference between an active and passive righteousness should help me, but I was still so filled with duty and how-to's that I could not understand his meaning. Understanding would come later, and with it a newfound freedom.

Grace Glimpses

In our presumption we suppress a great deal of the painful truth about ourselves. We can see sins in others and have the same sins in ourselves without recognizing it.

- Suppressing pain and doubt serves only to trap you in a vicious circle of spiritual blindness. You can begin to break this circle by opening up to God and sharing your deepest doubts—often in the presence of another whom you can trust and who is willing to accept you as you struggle.

Prayer: Lord, lead me away from my tendency to blame others for my problems. Give me a friend who knows more about grace than I do. Grant me the humility to open up honestly to you and another person about the hidden struggles of my heart. Amen.

3

Uncovering Deadly Patterns: The Sins of the Generations

We are something like an old painting that an artist has painted over. When the canvas is exposed to X-ray photography, hidden faces are revealed under the top layer of paint. That is why, when we try to get to know someone well, we want to meet his family. Here the hidden faces come into the full light. A person's family is not just his background, his context; it is an integral part of who he is.—Tim Stafford, *Knowing the Face of God*

Why had I done such a good job of pressing down my hurts and disappointments? One simple reason is that I was well trained. I had received from my parents so much that was beautiful: respect for authority, compassion for the weak, good manners, kindness, and self-discipline.

But not everything in my heritage was healthy. My inherited devotion to order, for example, was both a strength and a weakness. Order was virtually my parents' religion. In their view God was important, but order in life was paramount. And I was nurtured in their outlook.

Perfect Order

I was raised in a comfortable, carefully organized home in Daly City, a suburb of San Francisco. Our single-level house was nestled close to the base of the long, high mountain ridge that runs to the foggy Pacific Ocean. Our home was the picture of neatness. On the outside it was gleaming white with brown trim. It always looked freshly painted because my industrious father kept it that way. Inside my mother had its walls and floors scrubbed spotlessly clean.

My parents always spoke German to my younger sister Barbara and me, so I learned to speak German before English. It was a world with very few surprises in it, probably because most of our friends were German and orderly like us. As a teenager, I took the streetcar into San Francisco on Saturdays to the German school where I learned German grammar and culture. Here I developed most of my close childhood friendships, friendships that were stable and durable.

At home my mother was the perfect image of bustling loyal devotion to household routine. She went to church on Sunday, washed on Monday, ironed on Tuesday, mended on Wednesday, sewed on Thursday, cleaned on Friday, and did her food shopping on Saturday. If I forgot what day it was, I only had to watch what Mother was doing, and I knew the answer.

We had a highly disciplined lifestyle in other ways too. We didn't go into debt even in the darkest days of the Great Depression. Mother seldom bought anything for herself, and always made our clothes. We could even give food to our needy neighbors because of her careful management of our resources. Self-discipline was not just one value among many for us; it was our method for keeping life under control.

As a family we attended the nearby Presbyterian church, where I was a model pupil in the Sunday school. From my parents and the church I learned respect for the Ten Commandments. These commandments were not so much the Law of God as just a part of my family's religious moralism. God entered the picture as the authority figure whose task it was to keep life from slipping into chaos.

Behind this devotion to systematic living was a moral and religious outlook in which the operative word was *responsibility*. You paid *all* your bills on time, *never* went into debt, did the fair thing in business, and kept faith with your family and friends. This was the heart of my parents' moral order. Since our family could obey this dictum rather handily, we felt good about ourselves, and felt that God also approved of us.

Moralism versus Grace

It's not hard to see now that the implicit, working theology behind our "righteous living" was not really Christianity, with its doctrine of grace, but religious moralism. Such an outlook "exhorts a power of freedom that fallen man does not possess; it is a religion of control (called 'self-control') and not redemption, and it ends inevitably in despair rather than in hope. The moral imperatives exacted of men are predicated on a definition of sin as only willful and deliberate, thereby implying that the problem of sin is essentially superficial, a misconception that culminates in a false hope of self-justification."[1]

This outlook bypasses the need for God's grace as we attempt to get our lives straightened out by self-effort. It assumes that hard-working religious people, like the members of my family, have the moral capacity to do right, and hopes that one day our good works will outweigh our deficiencies on the day of judgment. In the meantime, our efforts subtly put God in debt to us: We keep his laws, and it is his responsibility to tilt the universe in our favor.

But for all my parents' strengths, they were unable to sustain their order and moral rectitude long-term. Eventually their own standards of rightness and justice led to the downfall of our family. When those standards were violated, they were unable to acknowledge wrong or extend forgiveness— the two things fallen people desperately need, and the two things self-righteous people cannot bring themselves to do.

Bitter Seeds Sown

During my parents' first years of marriage, my mother took a job cleaning houses. Since she came from an affluent home in

Germany, it was a major sacrifice for her to work in the homes of other people. She faithfully saved the money she earned, about two thousand dollars. Dad invested her money in the stock market along with some of his own funds. He did it without telling her about it.

When the stock market crashed in 1929, Dad lost all his investments, and Mother's money too. She felt betrayed by his failure to tell her that he had invested her savings in the stock market. When her money was lost, she felt deeply wronged.

Since we were all moralistic people—and "non-sinners" in our view—I don't think it ever occurred to my father to say to my mother, "I have sinned against you. Please forgive me." Dad avoided this kind of confession, and Mother did not confront him. Instead, she bottled up her bitter resentments against him. Neither of my parents were prepared to admit that they had a deep rift between them. The name of their game was push-it-down-and-don't-talk-about-it-so-that-it-will-go-away.

I too repressed my feelings at a time when an open discussion was desperately needed.

But the cost of this sort of self-deception is extremely high. By the time I was eight or nine years old, I felt there was something sad and odd about my mother. She would try to get me to eat more, but she would also constantly urge me to take laxatives without any reason. At first I argued with her, but she insisted, with a tone of fear in her voice, and out of respect for her I would take the chocolate laxative from her hand. I would then leave, ostensibly to eat the laxative. But what I really did was hide it behind my bed, and later flush it down the toilet.

As I grew older I resented and resisted my mother's overprotection. For instance, she wanted to keep me looking like a little German girl with blond braids arranged on my head or around my ears. I hated the idea of being dressed up like a German doll. I soon persuaded my understanding father to let me have a short cut and perm. When I came home from the beauty parlor and showed my mother my short curls, she cried.

My desire to learn how to do things around the house was also frustrated by my mother. In her mind, preserving order in the home was so important and the work had to be done so perfectly, that she never encouraged me to learn household tasks—to cook, or sew, or even to complete the washing of dishes if I didn't feel like it. I think she also wanted to keep me dependent upon her.

When I was about eleven, my mother's treatment of my sister Barbara increasingly upset me. Barbara had developed *petit mal* epilepsy. From then on, Mother treated her like an invalid who did nothing but play with dolls all day. I disliked seeing Barbara turning into a nonperson. The concept of codependency wasn't around then, but I knew something was wrong in the way Mother was encouraging Barbara to depend upon her. It made me so indignant that I think I hated my mother for her behavior. She was violating something fundamental in Barbara and in me, and by the time I was twelve I was pleading with my dad to do something about it.

Sometimes he tried to make changes, when it became apparent even to him that Barbara was turning into a wet dishrag. The following pattern developed. He would talk it over with Mother, and she would insist that she was right. He would blow up, and then in disgust retreat from the situation by ignoring it. It was passivity, fight, and flight, followed by "peace" achieved through the suppression of alienated feelings. Afterward we would all act as though nothing had happened.

I too suppressed my feelings—and the truth—at a time when an open discussion was desperately needed. Mother really did require help, and Barbara and I needed protection from her strange behavior. Dad's failure to ask questions—or to listen to me when listening might cause pain to all of us— unfortunately taught me to keep my innermost feelings bottled up. I had learned that facing up to truth in close relationships is unacceptable because it indicates that life is out of our human control.

The Waters Rise

But the inward floods continued to rise in spite of our family's game playing. One Saturday afternoon, when I was fourteen years old, all of our heavily sandbagged predictability was shattered, and a swarming deluge of muddy water poured into our lives.

My bedroom was also a big playroom that opened up to our back yard. I would often sit in front of the window with my feet propped up, reading my favorite Tarzan books. On this lazy sunny afternoon, a very uncomfortable feeling came over me. I jumped up, dropped my book, ran into the kitchen, and saw my mother. She had her head in the oven, and the gas was on.

Horrified, I ran across the kitchen and turned off the gas. I pulled my semiconscious mother away from the oven, opened all the windows, dragged her into the living room, and put her on the sofa. Trembling all over, I called my father at work and sobbed, "Daddy, come home! Mother just tried to take her life by turning on the gas in the kitchen."

It was a long, long forty-five minutes of waiting while Dad drove home through the busy streets of San Francisco. By the time he arrived she was sitting up, but very weak. Soon she was back at her work, carrying on as though nothing had happened. I was shaken by this tragic incident, but seen from today's vantage point, it was the aftermath that was most astonishing. Dad and I never sat down and discussed why my mother did this. I didn't ask any questions, and I was given no explanation.

A year later, on a Sunday afternoon, our family was sitting in a restaurant, enjoying a dinner of abalone fresh from the San Francisco Bay. While waiting for dessert, Mother got up from the table, went over to another table, and spoke to the diners in a low voice. They looked over at us, puzzled and annoyed. My dad then went to their table to find out what happened. They said, "Your wife said we were talking about her, and would we please stop."

After this happened several times, we simply stopped eating out. This was the beginning of isolation for our family. Dad's card party friends stopped coming to the house. Invitations to dinner became fewer and fewer, finally stopping altogether. Dad eventually gave up his duties in the German societies.

Mother's behavior became even more erratic. Sometimes she would fall to the floor in a faint; other times she would lock herself in the bathroom for hours. She began to hear voices and respond to them. Someone had to be with her around the clock. We did get her to start shock treatments at the University of California Hospital, but when Mother began to forget many good things along with the bad, she was frightened and wouldn't continue.

What had happened to my mother? When did it all begin? In Germany, she grew up in an affluent home where opera, ballet, and classical music were loved. When her mother died and her father remarried, she and her brothers were sent to different homes. The loss of a mother, the breaking up of her home, and starving in wartime were traumatic events she had buried deep. In her early thirties she was courted by my father from thousands of miles away in San Francisco, California. Coming so far to a foreign country, not knowing the language, and leaving her homeland were, I believe, contributing factors that led to so much bitterness when her hard-earned money was gone.

Though I don't know all the causes of her mental disintegration, these unsettling events probably contributed to it. When someone experiences huge upheavals as she did, and there is only a stern moral or religious base to lean on, then the effect can be disastrous.

I cannot minimize the destructive influence of this constricted religious outlook. She saw God's love and acceptance as conditional, dependent upon blameless behavior. Instinctively, then, she knew she had to defend her innocence at all costs. Since she had no pardon from God, she needed to work hard at self-protection and self-justification. She insisted that she had no need of forgiveness and saw no need to extend it to anyone else.

She built her own private mental world, and she walled out my dad from her life. She would rehearse the problem over and over. "Can you imagine? Let me tell you what Dad did." Then after her tale of Dad's guilt was completed, she would irrationally attack herself, blurting out, "You accuse yourself, you accuse yourself." She could not convince herself of her own innocence, either.

She saw God's love and acceptance as conditional, dependent upon blameless behavior.

That was the despair of a religious moralist who could no longer trust in the saving power of her own righteousness. But, since we all believed as she did, no one in our family could help her face the root of her suffering. We were "non-sinners" together, though that was far from the truth. We were living a lie. For Dad had wronged Mother, and Mother hated Dad, and sometimes I hated Mother for what she did to Dad and Barbara. But none of us said a word, and the suffering continued.

In the midst of all the chaos, my father and I struggled hard to re-establish family coherence. I was forced into the role of being my mother's mother, and together Dad and I managed and controlled her life. By assuming these roles, we avoided conflict. But neither of us faced the emotional price we were paying to keep order.

Dad had lost a wife, and I had lost a mother. We needed to face this painful, unyielding truth and to grieve over it. But instead, we acted as though she were somehow normal. We let her choose her course of treatment, exclude Dad's friends from our home, and ruin the emotional life of my sister. We simply detached ourselves from her, tuning out her psychotic "voices" and building protective barriers. This was how we kept life in control.

A New Start

In 1949, Jack Miller appeared in this disorderly orderly world with a proposal of marriage. We met at a conservative Presbyterian church in San Francisco. I had one year of college left, and he had more than two years to complete. Before I could say yes or no, I told him about my mother and sister. A young man I had been engaged to earlier had broken our engagement because he thought that our children might be like my retarded sister and that I would be like my mother.

But Jack just smiled and jumped in. "I love you; I want to marry you, not your family. I trust God's plan for our lives, and I don't see it as a problem."

Agreement came for me after I took a week to lay all of these issues before God. Everywhere I turned in the Scriptures, and all the talks and sermons I heard that week directed my heart to listen to God. He impressed on my heart, *Rose Marie, this is a faith journey.* What was uniquely different in my relationship to Jack was our ability to talk through major issues and agree on them before we were married. He felt that we should not use birth control, that he should finish his schooling, and that I should not work to support him. At my urging we also agreed not to go into debt, believing that God would provide for all our needs. Given our previous commitments, this would be no small undertaking!

For the first ten years, our marriage worked well. There were several reasons we were happy together. For one thing, we were very good friends. Then, Jack opened my mind to the Scriptures, to literature, logic, and history in a way that four years of university had not done. He also drew me into his love of nature. We liked camping in the wilderness, and for three summers Jack and I lived and worked on fire lookouts near the Oregon coast. We were confident people. We both felt strongly that God was for us and with us.

Having this spiritual unity, we found ourselves able to accomplish all kinds of nearly impossible things. In the first five years of our marriage we had four children, and we lived on a limited income while Jack went to school. It was a tough challenge, but one I enjoyed, as I saw God again and again provide food and clothes for our rapidly growing family. During these years Jack completed college and two years of theological seminary and began working toward a Ph.D. in English literature.

Together we had a deep devotion to our children. We nurtured them in the Bible and the Shorter Catechism. We taught them manners, and encouraged them in our love of learning and reading. Camping vacations in the Redwoods on the Eel River were a highlight of every summer.

Life was predictable. We made our decisions together. We were not going into debt, we had the same values for our children, and we were partners together in our goals for Jack's future: a college or seminary professorship.

Unwanted Changes

Then the unpredictable happened. After ten years of marriage, Jack entered the pastoral ministry. He did not talk through this decision with me—not in any thorough way. Soon I resented the unexpected direction our lives were taking. I wore the mantle of pastor's wife like *Macbeth's* "giant's robe upon a dwarfish thief." No way did I want to become the suffering saint modeling perfection to a congregation! But my view of submission was such that if I opposed this decision, I would be fighting against God. I felt trapped by Jack's decision and victimized by his calling from God.

Jack had a difficult church-planting pastorate, and his joy was eaten up by church problems; mine was eaten up by the inadequate salary we received and the "loss" of my husband to the church. Soon the bills were piling up. After two years, the church began to stabilize and grow, but the peace we had together seemed to disappear.

After our fifth child was born, a time of severe temptation moved quietly into my mind like an unobserved shadow. Six weeks after Keren's birth, Susan, an affluent friend, came to visit. It was May, and already the temperature was in the 100s. We tried to preserve the evening coolness by keeping all doors and windows open at night, and then closing them in the morning and pulling the shades to protect us against the heat.

After being in the house for two days she said with the best of intentions, "Rose Marie, this is unbearable. You shouldn't have to live this way. Your house is so hot I couldn't sleep last night. I can't even get a decent glass of ice water from your refrigerator. You should have a bigger refrigerator and some kind of cooling system." Susan's comments penetrated the frontiers of my mind.

A Dark Cloud Falls

I couldn't sleep that night. I was hot, and I was angry. I was angry at the church for giving us such a small salary. I was upset because we couldn't pay all our bills. I was angry at Jack for giving his time, energies, and attention to the church. When the anger cooled, I was left with a feeling that God my Provider had disappeared. My mind filled up with a dark cloud of bitterness. And I stuffed it all. I thought, *Susan is right. I shouldn't have to live this way. This is all Jack's fault.* Because it was never openly faced by me, this pent-up anger went deep, and over a period of years turned into bitterness that ate at my relationships with God and Jack.

Instinctively the walls went up. I distanced myself from the problems and lived a life of pretense. My coping strategies were exhaustion, allergies, passivity, and outwardly doing my duty. The passivity manifested itself in my thinking I had nothing to offer to anyone. Therefore I put my efforts into making my children and husband successful. What I didn't realize was that I had begun to mimic the protective strategies that had seemed to work with my mother.

Ten years of joyful partnership now turned into "submission" without joy. I didn't know how to admit my anger, worries, and deep anxieties. However, I continued to function outwardly. This may seem contradictory, but it really wasn't. I was simply living out the habitual coping strategy learned from my parents. You did your duty, even though your inner world was in chaos. Inwardly, an orphan mindset; outwardly the forms of responsibility.

The Fruit of Bitterness

Human beings and their relationships can be mysterious. I did not then see the parallel between my mother's becoming bitter toward Dad and my becoming bitter toward Jack. But it should be clear that parental examples are powerful. The sins of the generations are handed on to the children, and, often unconsciously, the children receive them without understanding what they are inheriting.

My coping strategies were exhaustion, allergies, passivity, and outwardly doing my duty.

But such bitterness in human relationships does not stand alone. As a rebellious victim I was blinded by the fact that bitterness in human relationships is also bitterness toward God. You cannot be bitter toward the creature without becoming bitter toward the Creator. It would be years before I saw this fact and grieved before God with a godly sorrow that leaves no regrets.

But this leads to an obvious question: Why didn't I grieve, first over my mother and later over my failed relationship with my husband? The answer lies in my self-protective religious outlook. As a religious moralist I understood grace as an add-on to my strength. I could not admit that I was flawed in my close personal relationships and needed powerful intervention from above. I was the self-dependent Pharisee. My primary supports were family tradition, an outwardly obedient religious life, and my proven moral character.

I had, in fact, missed the reality of my humanness and the flawed nature of fallen human relationships. I needed to grieve over the loss of my mother, and I needed to grieve deeply. I needed to admit that my mother's flight into insanity hurt me badly, and I needed to forgive her. However, I had allowed a root of bitterness to color my whole life, including my attitude toward God. I wanted him to release me from my predicament without his dealing with my self-centered love of control.

Was I a "caterpillar in a ring of fire," predestined by some iron law of the generations to repeat the sins of my parents?

 ## Grace Glimpses

M. Scott Peck has observed, "To come to terms with evil in one's parentage is perhaps the most difficult and painful psychological task a human being can be called on to face. Most fail and so remain its victims."[2]

- We become victims of sinful family patterns when we refuse to see them operating in ourselves. It is painful to come to this kind of self-knowledge. It means admitting that, in some areas, we have been sinful and/or deceived our whole lives.

- Avoidance of painful truth manifests itself in our always having to be right and being intensely defensive in the face of criticism.

Prayer: Our Father in heaven, grant me wisdom to understand my family sin patterns and the strategies I use to cover up and cope. Teach me to identify self-righteousness and other evil tendencies in my heritage. Give me the grace to renounce the evil in them, and to turn away from the tendency to blame my parents for the sins I have accepted. Amen.

1. C. F. Allison, *The Rise of Moralism* (London: SPCK, 1966), pp. 207-208.
2. M. Scott Peck, *People of the Lie: The Hope for Healing Human Evil* (New York: Simon & Shuster, Inc., 1983), p. 130.

Part II

THE ORPHAN BECOMES A DAUGHTER

Apart from me you can do nothing.

Jesus (John 15:5)

4

Coming to Despair: "What Is My Real Problem?"

*The thirst became so bad that she almost felt she would
not mind being eaten by the Lion if only she could be sure
of getting a mouthful of water first.*

"I daren't come and drink," said Jill.

"Then you will die of thirst," said the Lion.

"I suppose I must go and look for another stream then."

*"There is no other stream," said the Lion. It was the
worst thing she had ever had to do, but she went forward
to the stream, knelt down, and began scooping up the
water in her hand. It was the coolest, most refreshing
water she had ever tasted.*—C. S. Lewis, *The Silver Chair*

The intense examination of my family background opened
my eyes to many things, but nothing in this self-knowledge
brought me peace. Struggling with physical and emotional
exhaustion, I continued to insist that Jack listen to all my problems and solve them quickly. He was the dominant, rational
husband who had all the answers. I was the emotional wife
who vented her feelings because she did not like his answers.
It was a subtle game we were playing. He was the "master,"
while I took the role of "victim."

Then came *the* crisis. We were asked to take someone into our home who was needy and homeless. The person was desperate, but so was I. "I don't have it in me to take one other person into our home," I vented. When Don moved in I was angry at Jack for not listening to me, and for making a decision that I didn't feel I had the emotional strength to handle. Jack had thought this would only be a temporary arrangement, but as you might guess, it lasted several months.

As I feared, Don was immature, uncooperative, and unwilling to fit into the order of the home. Coming from an urban background, he was unaccustomed to mowing the lawn, raking leaves, and pulling weeds. His idea of work was to follow Jack around and talk for hours on the phone. But the yard work was his responsibility. In the past we had asked people to leave who had refused to fit in or who had made no effort to change. But Don truly had no place to go, and we didn't want to put him out into the street.

Many times I fled to the ivy-covered carriage house at the far end of our yard. Here I sometimes cried for one or two hours at a time.

Once more I was under pressure, and I fell into my well-worn pattern for handling problems. I became tense and introspective, suppressing my anger toward Don and Jack. Eventually my negative feelings ran riot. I was now in hasty flight, sometimes quite literally. Many times I fled to the ivy-covered carriage house at the far end of our yard. Here I sometimes cried for one or two hours at a time: tears of fear, self-pity, condemnation, and raging frustration. I would leave more exhausted than when I came in. But in all of this I never took a close look at my faith life or repented of any of my own sins—not, at least, for anything basic.

When the anger was vented, I was left with feelings of shame. For a long time I had suffered from the generalized guilt that can hang over the modern woman during midlife when her identity is being challenged by family, and by physical and emotional changes. But with Don's arrival my guilt grew stronger. I resented him as an intrusion into my life, and resented Jack as the cause of this intrusion.

Sensing my anger, Jack tried to reconcile Don and me. The three of us sat on our large back porch around the picnic table. The wisteria formed a purple screen for our private meeting.

"I think we need to talk over a problem," Jack said. But neither Don nor I had a thing to say. Conflict? Neither of us admitted a single problem. We were too ashamed to own up to our real feelings. Jack soon gave up in frustration.

Exposed by the Law

It was at this time that the Law of God—the law that was the measure of outward morality and order—confronted me in a whole new way. As my confidence in Jack and myself eroded, I was coming to experience what I now call the "power of the law."

The law says, "Love your neighbor as yourself" (Mark 12:31), and I was discovering the utter impossibility of keeping that commandment. I felt trapped by Jack's decision, Don's unwillingness to adapt, and my own fear of losing my reputation if I asked him to leave. But there was a deeper entrapment. Not only was my moral will power absolutely powerless when it came to loving Don, but my feelings were totally negative toward him. Where there should have been love and acceptance, there was a strong spirit of condemnation and hatred.

The image of my goodness was being tarnished before my eyes. I had grown up as the good child, one who seemed to keep the law quite easily. When I was small, I was so obviously good that the local minister's wife brought her daughter over to play with me, hoping that some of my "goodness" would rub off on her. As long as I could control my world, I felt OK about myself. At least I could quiet my conscience with busyness. But now my goodness was in question, and it was frightening.

Rose Marie, the hater. Was this what I had to offer God? Try as I might, I had nothing else to offer. My problem was that "sin, seizing the opportunity afforded by the commandment, deceived me" (Rom. 7:11). *I was deceived in thinking that the law itself had power to produce love.*

My earlier doubts had come from my woundedness. You don't question God's very existence unless you are deeply disappointed with him. A deeper issue, however, was that I could not perceive God's unconditional love for me. I only sensed that the law of God demanded far more than I could ever give. Love my neighbor as myself? How? Don gave me no strokes, took my work for granted, and did as little as possible around the house.

> *I could not love and accept a person different from me. I had discovered within myself the power to hate.*

I finally realized the fatal truth about myself: I could not love and accept a person different from me, especially someone who was working against me. I had discovered within myself the power to hate. The apostle Paul knew all about it. He wrote, "I found that the very commandment that was intended to bring life actually brought death" (Rom. 7:10).

I held on—almost desperately now—to my view of myself as the wounded innocent, still caught in the vicious circle of blaming my circumstances, reacting with negative feelings to these circumstances by flight, and then, by the analysis of my feelings, acting like a victim. I had not yet clearly seen my sin as being against God. It did not occur to me that my hatred of Don revealed that I was walking in darkness (I John 2:9). But God now used the law to make my self-analysis and my growing self-pity intolerable and, paradoxically, to give me faint intimations of hope.

I could not shake off the call of God to love. I only felt the compelling power of the law's requirement: Forget yourself!

Love your neighbor! Real guilt was now knocking at the door. I sensed the shameful truth that I hated someone who was made in the image of God. I had moved from the burden of generalized guilt to a recognition of a specific and real sin in not loving Don.

Certainly the law as commandment and duty had no power in itself to allay my anger, to change me, and to restore harmony with God. But it could and did begin to expose the games I played. From the law I learned that God had absolute standards, and good intentions could not meet the law's demands.

Public Explosion

But I had not yet given up the victim's last refuge: my almost unshakable conviction that Jack and devotion to duty should and could rescue me. I had trusted in Jack—along with my own teeth-gritting efforts—to save me. This idolatrous confidence was shattered one afternoon in Washington D.C. in mid-June, 1975. After spending some time in the National Gallery, I once again spoke to Jack about my problem with Don. We walked down the broad flight of steps outside the art gallery and crossed over to the lawn on the other side of the street.

"Jack, life is so busy at home that I have no chance to talk to you. Barbara is sick again, and I'm worried about her. I have so much to do. I feel so depressed over it all. Don is such a . . ."

I could see a look on Jack's face that I read as rejection. He said something like, "Not again. Am I a husband or a marriage counselor?"

That did it. I said, "I want you to listen. Why don't you do something about getting Don to be more responsible?" Jack held up his hands in a defensive gesture. He said, "Please, I am so tired of all your complaining. You are so negative."

Negative? What right did he have to say that! I lashed out furiously. "You asked me what I wanted to see changed in you, and as far as I can see you still don't listen. You will stay up at all hours to listen to others, but you just don't care enough to help me!"

"Please, just stop it!"

Our hearts were suddenly frozen in ice. I ran into the gallery, locked myself in a bathroom stall, and cried.

We had never exploded like this before with each other and in public. Both of us had lost control and spoken harshly. By the standards of many family arguments it may not have been much. Passersby would hardly have noticed, since both of us tend to lower our voices when we get angry. But angry we were. I know that if I'd had the money I would have left, taken the train home, and let Jack sit there and wonder what had happened. The thought of revenge was sweet. The whole weekend was ruined for me.

It is at this point in many marriages, Christian and non-Christian, that a partner will say, "What's the use. Nothing is working in our relationship. Am I destined to spend the rest of my life like this?" They feel trapped by responsibilities, duties, and their own inner longing for something more.

Only One Exit

Leaving my marriage was not an option for me. My need to stay and do my duty was too strong, and I was too proud and ashamed to get help. But I was beginning to tire of the role of victim. It now seemed stupid to blame Jack for all my problems. Wanting more honest communication, I quietly asked, as we drove home the next day, "Jack, why did you let Don stay with us when I told you it was too much for me?"

Eyes on the heavy traffic, Jack answered, "I am sorry. I didn't know what else to do. My thought was only to take him in temporarily. But no one else could take him. I really did try to find another home for him."

For the first time in a long while, I was able to identify with him in his trouble rather than just consider how it affected me. From that point on, I stopped pouring out all my problems to him. I understood that Jack was unable to handle my complaining that came across to him as an avalanche of unbelief. The tensions eased between us. I began to hate performing outwardly while inwardly lacking a heart for the work I was doing. This hypocrisy only led to guilt and condemnation.

This insight might seem small, but it was momentous. The stormy orphan saw a glimmer of light—hope for possibly a better way to live, and a first calmness entered my soul. The worst pain was yet ahead, but now it was healing pain. I was learning that no imperfect human being can ultimately meet another person's deeper needs.

Think of the human state as one of stubborn blindness. We will rely on everything but God. He in turn will prepare us for grace by closing our favorite escape exits until there is only one way left. Jack and I had passed through a midlife crisis. I had my first intimations of what real sin and guilt are all about. I still struggled with unresolved condemnation, but life was no longer a private hell for me.

Having faced the fact that I had no power to produce love, I began asking honest questions about my real needs. What was my real problem? Why couldn't I forgive and love others? What was keeping me back from God? Was pride my problem? Frustrations can cripple us or lead us to ask revelatory questions. We have a choice. A right response leads us to reject the role of victim.

I had learned better how to cope with my problems, even some deep ones. I had also come to have some insights into my powerlessness to fulfill God's law. But I had not yet seen that behind personal and family problems lie deep sin patterns that can only be dealt with by God's grace. It would be another year before the convicting power of God's Spirit revealed the depths of my self-righteous pride.

 Grace Glimpses

There are two kinds of despair: a healthy, healing despair and a self-destructive despair.

- Healthy despair drives you to drop pretenses and seek God from the heart. It ends with a real beginning—new life energized by grace.

• Unhealthy despair drives you into the role of
  victim, in which all responsibility is denied
  and blame is shifted to others. It ends with
  immobilization, intense self-preoccupation,
  and false humility.

Prayer: Our Father in heaven, grant me wisdom to know the difference between these two kinds of despair. Teach me how to draw near to you so I will walk before you with integrity and not be a victim of self-pity. Amen.

5

Seeing the Counterfeit: The Moralist Meets the Hooker

The broken of heart, who come in unworthiness
trusting in God's atonement, they alone are made
right with God.—Kenneth Bailey, *Through Peasant Eyes*

Most of us want quick solutions to our problems. We have more interest in immediate deliverance from pain than in what God wants to teach us through the pain. But the Father does not let us escape; he lets us alone until we become fed up with our own self-centered attitudes. *When a healthy despair of self sets in, then God begins quietly to breathe into us a new teachability.* This process began for me in the fall of 1975, during a sabbatical we took in Europe. We were accompanied by our fifteen-year-old daughter and her high-school classmate.

In early September we began our trip with a week's vacation in Ireland. We traveled through southern Ireland in a rented horse-drawn gypsy wagon. It looked like a small covered wagon, with the arching cover painted in broad white and red stripes. It was reasonably comfortable, complete with four bunk beds and a tiny kitchenette with stove and sink.

Soon we were rolling down an Irish road at the rate of about 3 miles an hour. At top speed. Whenever we came to a steeper hill, we all climbed out except the driver. The wagon then crept up the incline. At such slow times we picked blackberries on the way, occasionally chatting with an Irish farmer. Traffic was light, often nonexistent. Each night we camped in a farmer's pasture along Ireland's picturesque southern coast.

Even though it was early fall, the weather was often cool and rainy, not the best kind of weather for someone like me, with sinus infections and allergies. Early in the week I felt the onset of a sinus headache. The pain worsened through the day; aspirin did not touch it.

I asked Jack if he would pray for me against another sinus attack. We all gathered in a circle as the sun set behind stone hedges and rolling green hills. Jack prayed simply and quietly for God to heal me.

Almost immediately the headache went away and the sinus infection cleared. My feeble prayer had been for this one healing, but for years afterwards I had no allergy-sinus problem. In the past, I would often become depressed under stress, sleep long hours, and then come down with debilitating sinus infections. This physical healing anticipated momentous faith changes that were soon to come into my life.

These four months in Europe were a sabbatical from seminary for Jack. He planned to use the time to study and teach on the subject of justification by faith. After visiting and teaching in Northern Ireland, England, Belgium, Germany, and Austria, we headed south through Italy and across southern France on our way to the Reformed seminary in Aix-en-Provence.

Unsettling People

After traveling all night by train, we arrived in Nice. The golden sun of late autumn was painted on the cloud-free blue sky like it was the first day of creation. The temperature was in the mid-70s. The air seeming remarkably free from pollution. After getting settled in our hotel, Jack suggested, "It's such a beautiful day; let's go for a swim in the Mediterranean."

As we walked the half mile to the sea, I squirmed to see so many pimps, prostitutes, and their customers lounging about. I have been around people who were as tough as and perhaps more dangerous than these individuals, but there was something in the atmosphere that troubled me. By the time we had arrived at the beach, I was disturbed to the point of anger. What was bothering me?

I thought back over the women on the street corners, and I knew. I hated the widespread acceptance of evil as normal. Take just one example. In this lovely white city of the sun, no one seemed at all troubled by the teenage prostitutes. Some looked very young. The beach was rocky and the women were all topless. This too was accepted as normal by all the bathers. I was relieved when we finally left.

Elsa

That evening we ate our meal in a restaurant near our hotel. The tables, covered with red-and-white checkered tablecloths, were close together, and the dining room was filled with people. After we gave thanks, we forgot about the moral atmosphere of the streets and began to laugh and talk. But the issue suddenly became personalized in an unexpected way.

After dinner, Keren asked Jack to buy her and her friend Cindy a Coke. When Jack learned they were one dollar each, he said, "That's too much money." Keren set herself the task of reasoning the two extra dollars out of him, with much laughter and humor passing back and forth.

Jack was just reaching into his pocket for the needed francs when an attractive young woman at a nearby table leaned over with a smile. She said in excellent English, "Please, let me buy the Cokes for the girls." Jack replied, "Sure, if you want to! I can always use the help. These girls are big eaters and drinkers."

What came next was a real surprise. She said, "You are Christians, aren't you?" We nodded. "I could tell because I knew people like you in Holland. I went to hear David Wilkerson speak at the Youth for Christ meetings. I liked him and the Christians. They had happiness, and I felt that in you as you were all laughing and talking."

Then this well-dressed woman looked at us and said with precision, "Do you know what I do for a living?"

Neither of us said what we were both thinking: *You are probably a hooker waiting for a client.* But Jack answered quietly, "I think we know what you do for a living."

Her name was Elsa. "May I talk to you privately without the girls?" she asked. After we asked the girls to return to their room, she asked us pointblank, "Do you think there is any hope for me?"

After an hour-long discussion, we went for a walk together through the streets of Nice. What we had seen that afternoon on the beach was nothing compared to what Elsa showed us in the evening. She pointed out prostitutes on every hand, many of them the same ages as our two girls.

I believe the healing that God gave in Ireland began to restore my confidence that God was with me. I now had a new boldness and a fresh caring. When we stopped at a sidewalk café for some tea, I plunged right in. "Come back to the hotel with us. Tomorrow we take the train to Marseilles, and on to Aix-en-Provence. We have friends there who will help you. Since you like Holland, we can help you go to the Dutch L'Abri. This is a study center for people who want to know more about God."

Elsa struggled with the implications. "Am I willing to give up my expensive lifestyle? Can I start over and be forgiven?"

After a time we left the café and went back to our hotel. Casting my fears aside, I urged, "Elsa, come with us." With a nod and a smile, she made her decision. "I will go with you."

The Discovery of Grace

We decided that the only thing to do was to get Elsa a room for the night in our hotel, since she was afraid to go back to her own room for her belongings. I was afraid, too. Were we going to meet up with her "employers"? She might have been under the control of organized crime. What would they do to her? What would they do to us? Were we putting Keren and Cindy in danger? What did we really know about Elsa? Could this whole thing be a superb act?

The clerk at the desk looked at us strangely when we asked for a room for Elsa. We did our best to act like it was the most natural thing in the world to rent a room for a well-dressed young woman with no luggage. As we said good-night to Elsa, Jack gave her his Bible to read. I said to Jack as I drifted off to sleep, "I wonder if she will even be in her room tomorrow morning."

In the morning I went down to her room, fears mounting as I rapped lightly on the door. In a moment, though, there she stood, dressed and ready to go. Before seven o'clock we boarded the train to Marseilles. Jack and I were both edgy, fearful of pursuit.

Elsa was thinking of different things. As she seated herself, she said, "I didn't sleep much last night. At first I thought, *This is ridiculous.* I went to the window to look at the beautiful moonlight and the street. The street had a strong pull for me. It called me like the voice of home. I decided a new life was not possible for me.

"But I took the Bible, and it fell open to a place where I read my life story. It's a prophet's book that tells how women like

> *"But I took the Bible, and it fell open to a place where I read my life story. I felt like God had been watching me all the time."*

me practice their business. I was shocked. I felt like God had been watching me all the time. It told me just how I behave and make my arrangements. But it also made me think maybe God knew me and could care for me."

She asked if we knew where this passage was. We shook our heads. She said, "I just took the Bible in my hand and it fell open and there was the passage. Like this . . ."

The Bible fell open and she looked at it. Astonished, she said, "This is it." She read to us from the third chapter of

Jeremiah about the behavior of Israel the prostitute. After she finished, she said questioningly, "Perhaps your Bible naturally falls open to Jeremiah 3?"

"If it does," Jack answered, "that's news to me." He took the Bible in his hand and let it fall open several times. It never opened to Jeremiah 3.

When we arrived in Marseilles, we telephoned our friends at the seminary in Aix-en-Provence. They happily received Elsa as a guest and warmly welcomed us. After lunch I took Elsa out to a nearby arbor. With the warm afternoon sun filtering through the trees, I discussed the first four chapters of Romans with her. I had been fascinated with the book of Romans, still not understanding all it meant. But I did know that this was what Elsa needed to hear. I realized that she understood intellectually about grace, forgiveness, and Christ's death for her sins, but she simply couldn't accept the idea that God really loved her and could take away all her sins.

She simply couldn't accept that God loved her and could take away all her sins.

Elsa listened very carefully to all we said, but she had one more obstacle in the way of her believing. She said, in effect, "Everyone knows I am a sinner. *I know I am a sinner.* I have done many things for which I am ashamed. But there is also a great deal of pretense in me. I was a student in Prague when the Russians came and took over our country. I became a radical dissident, throwing stones at the police and soldiers. But I was really a hypocrite, a self-righteous hypocrite. I did not love my country; I just felt superior to other people and hated authority. I am the rebel through and through, and I love no one but myself."

You might not expect a hooker to confess that she was dominated by self-righteousness, but when grace begins to work, surprises happen.

Elsa and I continued to study Romans 8 together. She was attracted by its emphasis on "no condemnation." Full of sin and guilt, pride and self-righteousness, she soon found a release from condemnation. God forgave the rebellion of her heart and her fierce self-righteousness. Broken in heart, unworthy, trusting in the work of Christ, she was made right with God.

She was baptized in a little French Reformed chapel in Aix-en-Provence. In an interview with the church leaders, she told how she was astounded to discover what the Father had done in giving his Son for a sinner like herself. "What a big love God has when he can forgive and accept someone like me!"

I watched the ceremony with tears and afterwards embraced her as I would my own daughter. She had found the strength to leave her previous way of life, because the biggest problems of all—guilt and shame—were removed through faith in Christ.

The irony was not lost on me. I had really wanted to rescue Elsa, but had so little sense of how much I also needed to be rescued. Here I was, the moral self-righteous woman trying to find my way to peace through moralistic self-effort, leading a sinner to Christ. The difference between Elsa and me at this time was that Elsa knew she was a sinner. Under the surface I still had too much strength of the wrong kind and continued to deny the real sin and guilt. Instead, I took the stance of a victim, blaming Jack and my circumstances when life was out of control. Was finding peace that simple? Just repenting and relying on Christ's justification? The image of Elsa haunted my mind with hope.

Deeper Healing Begins

I believe Jack's prayer for me in Ireland did more than heal my sinus headache. The healing was going deeper, into the inner recesses of the self. Clouds of fear seemed to be lifting from my soul; hints of a more settled peace were felt in my life, and there was a hunger within me to know more of God's unconditional love.

Our encounter with Elsa was an important turning point in my life. You will note that much of my security was tied up with home and family. I was wonderfully confident in my own house; there I felt in control. I didn't mind washing up after all kinds of people and feeding them. I had some natural understanding of the psychology of human beings and was quite willing to make them conform to the rules of our household or the laws of the Bible. But I did not know how to go deeper into the lives of people. I did not know how to help them link their lives to Christ. Jack was the one who always taught them how to relate personally to Jesus. He talked much about "sonship." Most of this seemed to miss me.

But now that Christ had conquered Elsa, I was astonished at God's power to change this rebellious woman of the streets. I was surprised—and awed—by grace working in her life. The change in Elsa also gave me hope that God was powerful and that perhaps he could change even me. Soon I was going to be surprised by his grace—grace that would reach down into the core of my life.

Grace Glimpses

Religious moralism and Christianity are both concerned with obedience and standards; they are both involved in doing good.

- Religious moralism is rooted in the power of the will and self. Eventually it fails and we act like orphans: frightened, insecure people who need to be in control. We might be able to analyze our problems, but we cannot invent a cure.

- Christianity is rooted in the power of Jesus Christ. Eventually we come to rely on what he has already done about sin. We can still analyze our problems, but ultimately our hope for a cure rests on the grace that comes through our relationship with Jesus.

Prayer: Heavenly Father, send your Holy Spirit to penetrate to the core of my life. I know so little about grace. I really do act like an orphan when my life and relationships are out of control. Teach me about your unconditional love. Amen.

6

Finding Forgiveness: The Moralist Meets Jesus Christ

But this Christian righteousness is the greatest righteousness. . . . It has nothing to do with what we do or how hard we work, but it is given to us and we do nothing for it. . . . We receive and allow someone else to do all the work for us and in us, and it's God that does it. That's why we call it "passive righteousness."—Martin Luther, paraphrased from his *Commentary on Galatians*

David Mains reflected on the breakup of the well-known Circle Church, which he had pastored, in an article called "My Greatest Ministry Mistakes." Mains said that one of the chief causes of the split was an omission on his part: In all his years in the church, he never once preached about human depravity.

Mains implied that the church was fragmented because the leaders and the congregation were unprepared for their own capacity to sin. In a parallel way, my life was fragmented under pressure because I underestimated my human depravity. I not only denied my own capacity to rebel against God, but I also did not see my love of control as the outworking of rebellion.

God's ministry of grace to me began as he broke down the self-righteous defenses of an orphan/victim who refused to admit corruption in her life. Instead, when I felt guilty, I just got busy, read a book, tried harder, and even started reading the Bible more faithfully. One of the most serious of human faults is relying on ourselves instead of relying on God. There is nothing we give up more reluctantly than the feeling that *I can do it*. When that doesn't work, our natural impulse is simply to despair.

I believe it is impossible to face your hurts and hidden sins without the knowledge that God loves you. The burden is too heavy. Up to this point, my lack of awareness of God's unconditional love was the core reason I needed order and control. Grace to understand this truth must come to us on God's terms, not ours. It only enters our lives when we stop trying and cry out to our Father genuinely for help. I asked with a real hunger for an answer, "What am I missing?" My answer was on the way.

Lessons on the Ski Slopes

In early March of 1976, Jack and I went with thirty Americans to Switzerland for a conference in Chateau D'Eaux. While traveling by bus from the airport to the village, I caught my first view of the Swiss Alps, a spectacular backdrop to tranquil Lake Geneva. Magnificent!

We drove down a long, troughlike valley, with the chalets and homes of Chateau D'Eaux clustered casually about midpoint. As the big chrome and glass bus eased into town, we saw a high, walled knoll with a church and a small cemetery near the center of town. Off to our right loomed the Alps where the skiers went. A turn of the road and a short drive up the hill brought us to a small hotel. Here was our home for the week.

Jack was one of the speakers for the conference and spoke on the theme of sonship. Jack had learned much from patiently answering many of my questions: "Is God ever angry at the Christian? What is his attitude toward you when you don't do your duty? When your conscience condemns you, does this mean that God condemns you, too?" These questions prodded Jack to study Galatians and Romans to find the answers, and the fruit of his study was the theme of his talks that week. Another speaker was focusing on learning to forgive one another with the memory, from the heart, and with the mind and body. All of these were means used to prepare my heart for a powerful working of God.

In the middle of the week I walked into the village, rented skis and boots, and bought my ticket for the gondola that took me up into the Alps. It swung over the valley, over the tree-tops, and soon there was nothing but snow-clad slopes. Halfway toward our destination, we stepped out of the large gondola and into smaller ferris wheel-like cages that held two people. They carried us to the crown of the Alp. The view was breathtaking.

The Father had opened my eyes to grace . . . but it was a most painful encounter.

It was a brilliant day, with the sun shining and the snow a glistening white. I had a vision of myself sweeping down the side of the mountain with wonderful abandon. But then I took a second look at the mountain, and reality knocked on the door. Below me I could see ridges and humps of frozen ice. I was way out of my class.

God, how am I going to get off this mountain? I wondered. I'm not sure whether that was a prayer or simply a desperate cry for help. With my limited skill, there was no way I could ski down that slope. Yet it did not even occur to me to go back down the way I came up. Without another thought I pushed off. I quickly picked up speed and could feel my skis beginning to slip. Then I was falling over, and within a few yards I was down.

I kept repeating this pattern. I would get up, push off, pick up speed, and then slip out of control and fall. This continued until finally in frustration I took off my skis. As I was taking off the bindings, one ski slipped from my hand and went slithering out of my reach down the mountainside, picking up speed like a projectile.

I tried walking, but walking was even harder than skiing. In some places the snow was so soft that I sank down up to my knees. I even tried sitting on my rear and sliding. After three hours of plodding, falling, and getting up, I arrived at the gondola station. The last gondola of the day was ready to leave. I must have looked dreadful, because a Swiss skier immediately offered me her seat. Half an hour later, I walked wearily through the snow-covered streets of the village to the hotel, with my skis on my shoulders and my feet dragging in the stiff, heavy ski boots.

Jack met me at the door of our room, and I told him the long, sad story. He went into the bathroom, filled the tub with hot water, and helped me get into the tub to soak my tired body.

In my heart I blamed God for the whole ghastly episode. I railed, "Why did you let me go up that mountain when you knew what it would be like?" The idea that my attitude was one of blame-shifting arrogance—well, that had not yet occurred to me! But the following Sunday I received the answer to my question. I learned why God had permitted me to have this humiliating experience.

The Father's Kiss

As we gathered for worship that Sunday in a large room facing the Alps, I seated myself near the front in a comfortable chair. One side of the room was a solid wall of windows. The day before, twelve inches of new snow had fallen. It was a glorious winter wonderland.

Soon Jack was preaching about another glory, the greater glory of Christ. "He was broken for us, smitten for us like the rock in Exodus 17." Jack then described the "righteousness of God received through faith." I only half listened. "Trying in your own strength does not give you a living relationship with God. It is all a free gift through the merits of Christ. . . . Forgiving others is only possible when you know that the Father has forgiven you for Jesus' sake."

These words came floating through my reverie. I brushed them away, but this time they refused to leave. They kept hovering, waiting for an entrance to my heart.

I don't remember much from the rest of the sermon, but when it came time for communion Jack said, "The Lord's Supper is the Father's kiss, assuring us of his love." As the loaf of French bread was broken, it gave a crack. I saw with new eyes the spear of the soldiers breaking the body of Christ for my sins. My own heart broke as I remembered the ski incident of a few days before. It was as if God were saying to me, *Rose Marie, your whole life is like your slide down that mountain. You are full of presumption, self-righteousness, and pride. I let you go up there to show you about yourself.* There was no audible voice saying these words, but they were there, and directed to my heart.

The Father had opened my eyes to grace, the caterpillar was being lifted out of the fire by his loving hand. But it was a most painful encounter. The fire seemed to have entered my heart, burning away at my intense self-centered moralism.

The Dragon Skin Comes Off

I now realized how many times I had blamed God and others for the hard things in my life. I could see that my problem at Ruth's wedding had been caused by my pride. A proud self-sufficiency had kept me from accepting the offers from others to help with the food. I saw clearly that when my pride and self-righteousness got me into a mess, my natural reaction had been to blame God first, Jack second, and my circumstances third. Blame-shifting is crippling, because it disguises the real issues of sin and grace.

I love the Narnia tales by C. S. Lewis. In *The Voyage of the Dawn Treader,* the self-centered Eustace becomes a dragon. When he pulls off one dragon skin by his own efforts, there is always another tough layer underneath. My dragon skin was my self-righteous moralism. My so-called goodnesses were part of me. They were heavy dragon skins, because they were the protective armor that blocked me from knowing the love of God. The difference between me and Eustace was that I had not been trying to take them off. God simply stepped in. And with this intervention of the Father of grace, my dragon skin of moralism was penetrated. I had felt the ripping and tearing by the Lion of Judah. Now I wept tears of repentance with only one Kleenex to stem the tide.

My "Goodness" Is Not Good Enough

I was exposed and forgiven at the same time. I realized why I had had such a difficult time understanding Martin Luther's introduction to his commentary on the book of Galatians. He was writing to people who were *sinners*, who had no hope of any righteousness of their own.

Of course, like many typical modern Christians, I knew I had "sins." At least a few. But they were mostly surface things, matters of outward behavior, actions rather than deep attitudes. My whole way of thinking was centered on moral failure and moral success rather than on sin and grace. Before this experience of exposure, I thought of sin as a failure on my part or others'. I was inexorably condemned by these same failures, but I defended my shabby record by blaming others when things didn't go the way I wanted. Because I did not believe God loved me on the basis of Christ's life, death, and resurrection, I could not face the risk of seeing my sins as my own responsibility.

I was surprised by grace: The kiss of the Father had welcomed home the prodigal daughter.

Then, having tried to clear my conscience by blaming others, I turned on the afterburners and made myself busy with work and duty. Or to use Luther's language, I was full of *active righteousness.* I looked to my outward activity to feel good about myself, and judged others by my own active standards.

But here I was caught by my own conscience. All the decisions to go up the mountain and ski down were my own. Why didn't it occur to me to go down the way I came up? Well, that's how I lived my life. I was my own leader; I followed my own wisdom, relied on my own strength. To be sure, there were hard moments when even I could see I needed help. But I always wanted God to strengthen *my* strength and to enhance *my* good record. With a new clarity I saw in the communion that Christ had kept the law for me. The only worthwhile record was Christ's obedient life and his death for my sins. "Amazing love! How can it be that thou, my Christ hast died for me?"

Until now I had never really seen or admitted that I had neither strength nor righteousness. But at last I said to myself, *You keep toughing it out; you keep trying; you keep pressing on. These are good qualities to have if the underlying basis is faith. But if it is done simply out of self-effort, then you are bound to fail.*

Christ's Righteousness Is Everything

Now I understood what Luther was talking about: "In the righteousness of faith we work nothing, we render nothing to God, but we only receive and allow another to work in us."[1] This is what he called a *passive righteousness*—a righteousness that is credited to our account through faith. This was Christ's righteousness, bought with the price of his blood on the cross. This I received by faith. The reason it had been so difficult for me to have a personal faith in Christ was that I had not experienced total forgiveness. But I had now brought real sins—including my attitudes of self-dependence and blame shifting—to a real Savior, and they had been forgiven.

I was so deeply convicted of my sin against God and awed by his receiving love that I barely made it through lunch that day. How awesome it is to be loved unconditionally by a holy, righteous God. I couldn't wait until I was alone with Jack to tell him all that had happened.

Imagine the look on his face when I threw my arms around him and told him I was a sinner! Weeping on his shoulder, I asked his forgiveness for the spirit of pride, condemnation, and judgment I had brought to our marriage. He forgave me with great joy. It was a sweet reconciliation.

I certainly didn't have a full grasp of all God offered me as his daughter. But on that ski slope sin was exposed—my proud, independent spirit—and at the Lord's Table I saw the meaning of Christ's death. I was surprised by grace: undeserved, yet freely given. It came to me with almost burning certainty that he loved me and died for me. The kiss of the Father had welcomed home the prodigal daughter.

Controlled by Grace

Was this a conversion experience? Many people have asked that question. I am not certain. I had known all the right Christian words. And I had prayed and had seen answers to prayer, especially in matters of health, protection, and material provision for our family. But before Switzerland my working religious outlook does not seem to have been generated by grace. Below the surface, mine was a religion of self-control through human will power, and my primary interest was in self-justification, not in Christ's justification. But whether this was first-time redemption or a major spurt in grace, the principle remains the same. The gospel is a power in the lives of those who know they need the blood of Christ as a present power.

My problem was that I had been actively trying to build a good record through moralistic effort. Order and control were so important to me because I believed they provided the only possible basis for establishing a secure standing with God. Now all of this "active righteousness" was under the blood of Jesus. The only condition for justification is the recognition of one's need of it; knowing that your very heart of hearts is sinful—an old-fashioned conviction of sin.

Give up your success-and-failure patterns. Seek grace in Christ, humbly and honestly. Understand that a conviction of sin does not make you neurotic, but rather it spells the beginning of the end for neurosis. After all, what is a neurotic? Simply a hurting person who is closed off to criticism in any form and yet engages in the most intense, destructive self-criticism that produces neither hope nor help.

What a marvelous relief God's grace in Christ offers. I had been totally criticized, and at the same time I was completely forgiven. As I rested in the work of another, my heart was at peace with God; and for the first time, I felt at peace with myself.

Grace Glimpses

Faith in the gospel—Jesus' atoning death on the cross and his resurrection—is what brings us to Christ, and what motivates us for growth in grace.

- Faith and presumption (reliance on self and outward morality) look so much alike that only crises can expose presumption for what it is. Presumption constantly tries to shift our reliance on Christ's righteousness to our own efforts.

- Therefore, crises become God's means of forcing us to turn away from circumstances, feelings, and our own strength—and to turn toward God.

- Growth in Christ is not rooted in moralistic will power. It is only possible as we are trans-planted by faith, through the power of the Spirit, into the soil of grace.

Prayer: Our Father in heaven, please show me the difference be-tween real faith and a demanding presumptive faith—so I can put my trust in Christ alone. I am so easily blinded by wanting to look good to myself and to others. May the gospel of the Cross and the resurrection of Christ be a continuing power in my life. Amen.

---

1. Martin Luther, "The Argument of the Epistle of St. Paul to the Galatians" in his *Commentary on Galatians* (see appendix A).

Part III

THE LIFESTYLE OF A TRUE SON OR DAUGHTER

Bear with each other and forgive whatever
grievances you may have against one another.
Forgive as the Lord forgave you. And over
all these virtues put on love.

Colossians 3:13-14

7

Forgiving Others:
The Key to Peace

By forgiving us, [God] changes our past. By promising, he secures our futures. By his grace we participate in his power to change the past and control the future. We, too, can forgive and must forgive. We, too, can make a promise and keep it. Indeed, by having these two divine powers, we become most powerfully human and most wonderfully free.—Lewis B. Smedes, "Forgiveness: The Power to Change the Past" in *Christianity Today*

Soon after our return to Jenkintown in March of 1976, Jack found himself drawn reluctantly into a controversy at the seminary over justification and good works. The discussions were wearing for him, but they kept driving him to study the Scriptures. He especially received help through the study of Galatians 4:4-7. His mind was captured by verse 7: "You are no longer a slave, but a son. . . ." He gave the language contemporary expression by substituting the words "an orphan" for "a slave." Jack's insight was far from clear to me, but I did hear the expression "no longer" and sensed that it meant that justification by faith created a whole new situation for life.

New Freedom in Forgiveness
During this time Jack met with Barbara and asked her to forgive him for his failures and sins as a father. He then forgave her in turn for things she had done against him. I was not at

their meeting, yet I could tell it had been a profitable encounter. Jack came home exhausted, but remarkably relaxed and at peace. This mutual forgiveness broke down a barrier between them. I was impressed. I could see that being forgiven and forgiving others opened up lives and built communication where there had been deep estrangement.

This encouraged me to take my first fumbling steps to live out the new freedom and forgiveness that I had experienced in Switzerland. The knowledge that God loved me, and that he had forgiven me completely while knowing me perfectly, was filtering slowly through my soul. As it did, I began to look at my life and relationships without automatically fearing condemnation for the failure and sins they might reveal in me.

God's approach was wonderfully simple: Break out of your defensive isolation by changing the object of your trust! I now did that.

I deliberately moved from relying on myself and my self-centered efforts. I said, "I cannot change my tendency to suppress my pain and isolate myself from others, but Christ can help me. I will now depend on him to guide me."

In some sense the believer is always a caterpillar in a ring of fire. It's just that now you can pray and ask for grace to do the impossible. You are no longer the religious moralist fighting the success/failure conflict. You now know that the fight based in human will power has already been lost. You also know that as a child of the Father you are fighting the battle that has already been won for you by Christ. The struggle to establish a good record is ended, but the struggle against "the sinful nature and the devil" has just begun (Rom. 10:1-4; Gal. 5:6, 13-26; Col. 3:1-11).

This approach to life seems vaguely pious and unworkable for many Christians. Sometimes the hurt is so deep that forgiving the other person appears impossible. This is especially true if the person who has offended is not repentant. To forgive under such circumstances doesn't appear to make sense—and it's certainly not "fair." How can you forgive when everything inside you shrieks out that you have been wronged? Well, don't sell Jesus short! See what he enabled this caterpillar to do.

A Change of Pattern

A surprise visit from my daughter Barbara touched off a new conflict for me. I was in the laundry room on our second floor, folding clothes when the doorbell rang. I went downstairs and found Barbara standing at the front door. It took me a moment to take in the scene. Always slender, she now looked just thin and sick. Her face was drawn and waxy white. Dark blue smudges underlined both of her eyes.

I welcomed her as she mumbled, "Mom, I'm sick." She asked me to take her to our doctor. She was diagnosed as having mononucleosis. From the doctor's office I took her to the house of one of her friends.

I was glad that she had come to us when she didn't feel well, but a few days later, my heart sank when I heard that Barbara had flown to St. Thomas Island for an extended vacation with a new boyfriend, John. John was a high-powered drug dealer, the antithesis of everything our family stood for. Once more I was deeply disappointed. When she returned from St. Thomas, she was wearing heavy gold rings and bracelets that John had bought her. Soon she was sporting an expensive fur coat.

Until now, when something difficult like this had happened, I had become angry, backed off and felt guilty, suppressed my guilt and anger, and wound up depressed. In my introspective sadness I would become passive and see myself as the victim, the wronged righteous moralist in a world of sinners. It was the old fight, flight (retreat in anger), and suppression (guilt and sadness) pattern that I had refined into an art form.

At this juncture with Barbara, I felt myself sliding into this pattern once again. And I believe Satan was working to encourage me in this direction. He was saying, *Rose Marie, it isn't any use. Just give up.*

But for once he overplayed his hand. The crisis was so glaring that even I could see that I had to fight in a new way.

Who knows exactly how the Spirit works in the unconscious life? Sometimes he makes us hungry, thirsty, and dissatisfied with our reactive habits, knee-jerk thinking, and frightened living. We begin to catch a view from Scripture—however vague—of life as God wants it lived. Then the inward ear begins to listen as Jesus tells us about beautiful things that, by ourselves, we do not understand.

What beautiful thing did God have to show me this time? I found myself wanting to forgive Barbara. Grace now surprised me by its calm, freeing beauty. Here, for the first time, the reactive pattern so characteristic of my life was replaced by another pattern. Instead of fight and then flight, I was overcome by a deepening forgiveness. Now that's grace.

Like Mother, Like Daughter

Grace was not a sentimental denying of the facts of my own life or Barbara's. Instead of fleeing into denial, I now took a long, hard look at Barbara. For the first time I saw that maybe she and I had more in common than I had ever suspected. For example, she seemed to be completely blind to her habit of wounding me and others, just as I had once been blind to my own sins.

I also saw that she liked the role of the victim who is persecuted by "authority figures." There too we had a lot in common. Had she learned from me to cast herself in the role of the passive sufferer, the one who is always right and being wronged by "others"?

The lights were going on. I had never heard Barbara confess that she had done anything wrong. Had she inherited this pattern of acting and reacting from me?

That evening at dinner I said to Jack, "You know, I don't think Barbara has a clue as to how much pain her behavior has caused us. She really is hardened through 'sin's deceitfulness'. She only sees us as damaging *her!* And yet she keeps coming back when she gets sick."

As I talked, my perspective on Barbara began to change. Only in recent months had I understood that *my* self-centered pride and self-righteousness were sins against God. Maybe that was the root of Barbara's problem, too.

In my own life, I had been spiritually derailed by this moralism, and I had passed it on to our children as well. By moralism, of course, I don't mean "morality" or "morals," which are fine, but the standpoint of self-righteousness adopted by those who can conform outwardly to God's laws and human standards. Outward conformity obviously hadn't worked for Barbara. It hadn't worked for me, either, but only now was I becoming honest enough to admit it. I sensed that the way I closed myself off from others—and even my own conscience—was a reflex of rebellion, expressed in intense self-righteousness.

Later, I went upstairs to settle a conflict between my mother and my sister Barbara. I came face to face with their refusal to admit wrong. My mother said, "I am not talking to myself!" Barbara was sobbing, and very angry, yet denying it. Finally I got them calmed down and reasonably reconciled. I was horrified by their mutual blame shifting and denial of wrongdoing. Here it was again—the same blinding power at work in my mother, my sister, my daughter, and me—the endless repetition of the same foolish patterns of behavior and, in the process, the shifting of blame onto others (Gen. 3:1-13).

Such a self-righteous outlook is only possible if you deny the inner compulsions of the mind—where the real person lives and desires. I am talking about "that fallen human nature touched in every area of life by the deforming presence of original sin. . . . Apart from grace our best actions are still built upon the foundation of unbelief, and even our virtues are organized as weapons against the rule of God."[1]

How Can I Fight Such an Enemy?

Jack often says in his paradoxical way, "There is great power in negative thinking of the right sort." He means that hope is born in those who admit the depth of their need. That's what I was now seeing. The more I saw the depths of self-righteousness in myself, the more I felt the greater depths of God's love to me.

A few nights later, I said to Jack, "I want to forgive Barbara."

"I thought you already had," he replied.

I explained, "I mean in a different way . . . like the way God has forgiven me. You know, totally and unconditionally. Remember what James [a friend of ours and a Bible teacher] said about forgiveness: 'Do you forgive with your heart, your memory, your body?' Forgiveness of others has to be a total thing. Let's do that together now for Barbara."

We had a time of prayer, after which Jack said, "I think a deeper understanding of the evil in every one of us makes us more compassionate. We see that we are all in the same sinking boat."

The more I saw the depths of self-righteousness in myself, the more I felt the greater depths of God's love to me.

"Jack," I said, "I believe I have been blind in my approach to Barbara. I have been stymied by the lack of change in her despite all our prayers. The more we pray, the more she deteriorates. I have been aware of my feelings of disappointment and hurt, but I wonder if I am unconsciously condemning her and she feels it. Maybe my prayers for her have a hidden negativism in them—you know, a despairing feeling that she will never change."

It was a weighty thing to consider. Had we, in our praying for Barb, been ignoring the key of grace that can unlock the heaviest door and let in the light of God's love? We repented that night for letting Barbara's rebellion condition our thinking about her future. *Her negativity had influenced us to pray for her without confident hope.* We had been letting her evil define our response, and that was wrong. From that day forward, we began to pray for her with new confidence. We trusted that Christ was pursuing her through our prayers. Through faith we had a new freedom to expect that God would work in her life. God released us from the spiritual blindness that had kept us obsessed by her rebellion and our fear that she would never change.

Keys to Forgiveness

Praying became my most powerful resource, because now I was praying with the confidence of a daughter familiar with real grace. It is a liberating thing to see that grace is more powerful than all our distorted perspectives and our inherited patterns of twisted motivations. I could now pray for Barbara with hopefulness and a forgiving heart. And forgiving hearts are hearts that pray with power!

Let me summarize some basic discoveries that will transform our human relationships:

• You cannot forgive others from the heart without having come to a humbling knowledge of your own depravity and your inherited patterns of action and reaction.

It is a liberating thing to see that grace is more powerful than all our distorted perspectives.

• God's grace is a power at work on the inner life; once you are forgiven completely, you want to forgive others in the same way. Forgiveness is a process that is not automatic or easy, but it is possible through the Holy Spirit's work in us.

• You sustain the process of forgiving others by considering your own forgiveness in Christ.

• The struggle to reject negativism is also ongoing, as you pray for those who have deeply hurt and disappointed you.

• You forgive others from the standpoint of hope, expecting that in his own time, the Spirit of grace will work change in their lives through your prayers.

With these principles in mind, Jack and I began to approach Barbara with new freedom. Not long after this, the

front doorbell rang again. Jack answered and there was Barbara, standing in her expensive fur coat, again looking pale
and feeling sick. Jack took her in his arms and hugged her
warmly.

"Dad," she said, "pray for me. I don't feel well." But this
time Jack responded with, "Barb, I'll pray for your healing on
one condition: you let me pray for God to make you holy—
clean on the inside."

She stood there thinking, slowly and silently turning it over
in her mind. Finally she said, "You can pray that for me."

Jack then prayed that God would make her holy and
healthy through the riches of his grace. From then on, Barbara
came home more often, and she used the back door like the
rest of the family. Her health soon showed remarkable im-
provement. That too brought healing and hope to me.

🐦 Grace Glimpses

The normal Christian life is the life of grace expressing itself in
forgiveness.

- Even when our practice is subnormal, we
  must never accept an unforgiving lifestyle as
  normal.

- The Father wishes for us to see the beauty of a
  life of forgiveness—of being forgiven by the
  Father and of ongoing forgiveness of others.

*Prayer: Heavenly Father, grant me your grace to forgive those
who have wronged me. Forgive me for not believing they will
change. I bring to you my self-righteous attitudes. Enable me to taste
afresh your complete forgiveness. Amen.*

---

1. Richard Lovelace, *Dynamics of Spiritual Life* (Downers Grove, Ill.: InterVar-
sity Press, 1979), p. 86.

8

Dealing with Inherited Sins: Family Forgiveness

To come to terms with evil in one's parentage is perhaps the most difficult and painful psychological task a human being can be called on to face. Most fail and become its victims. Those who fully succeed in developing the necessary searing vision are those who are able to name it. For to "come to terms" means to "arrive at the name." As therapists, it is our duty to do what is in our power to assist evil's victims to arrive at the true name of their affliction.—M. Scott Peck, *People of the Lie, The Hope for Healing Human Evil*

Responsibility, decency, respect for authority, and devotion to family—these are all qualities that make up a wonderful heritage. These valuable elements were part of my family background, and in some measure had passed over into my life. I have always been thankful to my parents for these features in my family tradition. At the same time I was increasingly troubled by my family history. Was this a negative restlessness? No, it was like a newborn faith stirring in me. Faith has a contentment side, but sometimes it has in it a holy restlessness. It calls the self to leave behind old clothing that no longer fits.

Family Heritage—the Good and the Bad

I had been nurtured in a religious outlook that confused moral will power with faith, and substituted outer conformity for inner righteousness. Ignorant of the healing power of grace, the members of our family clung tenaciously to life with their moral strength until relationships became unendurable. The pattern typically was one of fight followed by flight into isolation. This was the "wall-building" I had practiced so instinctively all my life.

After Switzerland, I was sobered by the thought that the sins of the fathers sometimes are handed down to the third and fourth generations. I had developed a healthy fear for the kind of influence I might be having on my own children. What superficial and destructive attitudes had I handed down to them? I was thinking especially about the blinding effect of my self-righteousness.

Light dawned in my soul after reading Catherine Marshall's book *Something More*.[1] One evening in mid-November of 1976, the weather had turned colder and Jack built a fire in the living room. Warmed by the blazing logs, I pulled Marshall's book off the shelf. I turned to her chapter called "The Law of the Generations."

"Jack, listen to this." I read, "It is the nature of sin to divide, to build walls, resulting in strained relationships or estrangement."

I thought about the walls I had built in relationship to my mother over the years. At a glance you might not think this was true. Her mental world was so irrational and so totally divorced from reality that for a long time I could see no connection between her life and mine. Wasn't I right to have rejected the kind of relationship that today would be called codependent?

I have no doubts about the rightness of my refusal to enter my mother's psychotic world. But human life is not always simple. People often become like their parents in ways they may not recognize—in spite of their determined efforts to be nothing like them.

Even as a child I would not cooperate with or support Mother's anxieties and delusions. But having refused to be pulled into her paranoia, I developed protective strategies which, ironically, in some ways mirrored hers. She had constructed barriers to keep others at a distance, and I built mine to keep her far from me. I did not want to be controlled by her and her problems.

I had learned from my mother to protect myself by building walls. When she continually was out of control, I became deeply angry, but suppressed it. In the same way, I felt my life slipping out of control when Jack went into the pastorate. My coping strategy was to becoming angry and bitter and to build walls in my relationship with him. In my anger I thought, just like my mother, *My husband has betrayed me. This betrayal hurts me deeply, and I will not give him the opportunity to do it again. I will withdraw from him to protect myself.*

I had made a choice and asserted my independence against Jack—but I did it at a very high cost to myself and to him. I had taken the easy way out. I did not know how to work through our alienation. The will to defend myself saved me from my mother, but that same will to independence had subsequently threatened to destabilize my marriage.

Today we stress the importance of rejecting codependency, but we often overlook the fact that *rejecting a wrong kind of relationship does not necessarily mean that you have found the right one.* You still need to know how to love the person who is a threat to you.

Coming to Terms with Family Weaknesses

Some of these thoughts came to me that night as I read Marshall's book. I said to Jack, with one of my famous sighs, "I have passed these 'walls' on to my own children." I was thinking of my lack of honest communication with him, of my outer shell of moral behavior, and of my independent, defensive style in handling conflicts. Jack looked sympathetic and said little.

I was seeing my family's past with a new vividness; it made me groan. How little important communication went on in our home while I was growing up! Not even my mother's attempted suicide was discussed. Mother showed very little affection for me; seldom, except for a good-night kiss which was my duty to give, was there any display of love between us. Order was the ultimate value.

I knew now that God wanted me to take a stand by faith against my inherited legalism and the unforgiving condemnation that went with it. I said to Jack, "I really believe that the sins of the fathers and mothers get handed on to the children—along with the good qualities. I want to stop any sins from my family ancestry from being handed on to my children and their children—and to hand on the good qualities. I want to give thanks for the good my parents did, and forgive the evil."

Jack tended the fire and finally spoke. "I have my own sins that I passed on to our children—sins from my family heritage, like willfulness and dominance. It's no easy matter."

People often become like their parents in ways they may not recognize—in spite of their determined efforts not to.

But that night, God's Spirit led me to do what was not natural or easy for me. I had a strong, inward desire to have forgiveness prevail in all my family and to have forgiveness define it for the generations to come. It was as though the Father said, *Rose Marie, forgive as I have forgiven you. Accept as I have accepted you.*

I went into the kitchen to make us a pot of tea. As I waited for the water to boil, I called to Jack, "Will you please put on the record of the *Messiah?*"

I came back to the living room with a tray of tea and fresh baked cookies. Strains of "Comfort ye, Comfort ye, My People" came from the stereo. I poured a cup of tea for Jack, put some cookies on his plate, and continued to reflect on my past.

"I know my mother's negative chemistry affected me deeply. It's unconscious, but it's there. When the stock market crash swept away her money, she was totally mastered by a root of bitterness. I have never seen anyone more controlled by inward hostility. She hated my dad. It ate her up on the inside until it destroyed her sanity.

"But Dad did not seem to know how her negativism influenced the whole family. Or maybe he didn't want to face the shame of it all. This has been the unacknowledged dark shadow over all of our lives. Her life message to me was get angry, retreat, harbor hostility, by-pass your husband, and give yourself to your children as an escape. I want to have any bitter feeling removed from my life and the lives of our children and grandchildren."

Until now I had been too embarrassed to talk about these issues at any depth. I discovered that I was angry with Mother, too. She had poured all those sick energies into my sister and almost destroyed her. She rejected my father physically and emotionally, slept in a separate bedroom, and did not welcome him into it. My poor, dear mother! In her terrible isolation she was oppressed by her guilt and constantly accused by mysterious inward voices condemning her.

Need for Forgiveness

Now I needed to forgive her—not only for what she did to my father and sister, but for her overprotection and control of me, which expressed itself in a lack of love and affection. I especially needed to forgive her for her attempted suicide when just the two of us were alone in the house.

"I never heard my mother say she was wrong or sorry about anything," I said to Jack. "*I* can't remember saying to our children very many times, 'I am wrong; I am sorry.' I've never heard Barbara just say out and out, 'I am wrong.' "

"Jack, I need to forgive my parents!" The words and music from the *Messiah* broke into my painful story. "Cry unto her, that her warfare is accomplished, that her iniquity is covered." I believed the words, and in believing there was not only power to receive forgiveness, but to give it. *This is indeed the deepest comfort—to be accepted by God, totally forgiven, and then by grace to forgive the deepest wounds and hurts.*

A few days later, I made a bold proposal. "Jack, let's go to our children and their spouses and ask their forgiveness. I want a deep oneness to be in all of us. I want our whole family to be without walls."

I read again from Catherine Marshall's book: "I brought to the light all remembered dark heritage from previous generations. I had to forgive my ancestors and release them from my judgment." I was especially impressed by what I read next. Catherine Marshall asked her son to pray that God would release her from the evil found in her life from the heritage of her past. The author's final step was to praise God for hearing this prayer.

No Simple Matter

Jack's response was, "Let's slow down a minute and think it through. That's a big, big order, to pray that way with faith. How can I handle my remembered dark heritage from previous generations? I need the kind of self-forgetting and openness that only the gospel can give."

He was right. No method, no counseling strategy, can erase the dark heritage of any human being. Jack continued, "Remember those conflicts we had a couple of years ago? We condemned each other, and then we condemned ourselves. We did it as instinctively as we eat and drink. In any conflict between us, my first impulse still is to criticize you and defend myself, and then afterwards, almost unconsciously, to torture myself for being such a fool. It's terrible."

> *I can't remember saying to our children very many times, "I am wrong, I am sorry."*

He said with deep emotion, "It is especially hard for me to go to my grown children and say even about my surface sins, 'Right here and here I have sinned against you. I now ask for your forgiveness.' But this is probably small stuff. If I find dealing with my obvious dirt so painful, what will I do with all the sins that my family has swept under the rug for generations? I'm thinking of the deeper evils that I know must be in me and my family. I'm thinking of self-centered arrogance, feelings of superiority over other people, willfulness, blindness, and coldness of heart."

His frankness and depth of feeling did not overwhelm me. I liked it. "It's the honest man in you talking," I said. "We both desperately need 'something more' if we are going to do that kind of search into our lives."

I knew that the "something more" we needed was a more self-conscious resting on the gospel of grace. It was ironical. I was still such a spiritual toddler. I would have had trouble clearly defining justification by faith for you. I knew little about union with Christ and the implications of that relationship for growth in grace. But after my time in Switzerland I began to have a certain instinctive "feel" for how grace did not work and how it did. Grace works powerfully in the life when we forgive as we have been forgiven. I had been freely forgiven by God through faith in Christ's death, and now I could freely forgive other people.

Grace works powerfully in the life when we forgive as we have been forgiven.

The Weakness of Human Love

For the first time I was seeing how conditional our human love and forgiveness were. We love and we forgive, but then new wrongs take place, and we lapse right back into our unloving, condemnatory attitudes. Instinctively our judging minds think, *He (or she) knows better*, or, *I don't deserve to be treated this way.*

Meanwhile, theological differences over the nature of grace had intensified at the seminary where Jack taught. Caught up as an unwilling participant in the conflict, Jack was finding himself humbled in every area of his life. The long, complex debates at the seminary compelled him to give up his own wisdom and turn more to God's. Through the difficult time with me and Barbara, he was learning that the deepest wisdom comes to those who admit they don't have it—that "grace runs downhill to the humble." In all of this self-emptying, he was coming to experience more fully the love Jesus extends to us at the cross.

So, pushed and pulled by grace, we were now ready to bring forgiveness to our family as the gift of God. Jack summed it up: "God will hear our prayers for our family. But we *must* base it upon faith in Christ. For the only thing that can cancel out the condemnation of the 'Law of the Generations' is the work of Christ. He alone 'redeemed us from the curse of the law by becoming a curse for us' (Gal. 3:13)." We often think too narrowly of the gospel and its powerful implications. We see it as the only basis for our salvation when we first believe, but then we leave it behind us as a happy memory with little present relevance.

What do we *really* believe? That we are justified by faith alone in the gospel of Christ, but from then on, it's pretty much up to us to accomplish our sanctification. *We fail to see that being made right by God happens through faith, and growth comes through faith also.* The faith that saves is the faith that sanctifies, because it rests alone on Christ and his work.

I asked God for grace to forgive the sins of my mother and father. I also asked forgiveness for the sins that I had accepted from them and had allowed to become self-deceptive strategies in my own life. From my father I had learned to avoid conflict and honest communication. From my mother I had learned that control in life's situations is important, that withdrawal is a way of life, that we are victims, and that we have a right to bitterness if someone has wronged us.

I brought these sins to God and asked his forgiveness—on the basis of Christ's atoning sacrifice. After prayer I knew I had been forgiven. Naturally, this helped me feel better about myself and my family. But of greater significance was the new way I was operating; now I was thinking and moving in the context of God's kingdom of love.

During the next six weeks, we went to four of our five children and asked them to forgive us, as Jack had done with Barbara earlier. Some of these visits were painful. When we met with Jim and Roseann, we gathered around our dining room table. I cried and Jack looked a little embarrassed. But we confessed our sins to them, and they forgave us. Then they knelt by the side of the table, and we put our hands on them and blessed them.

As we went to our children, they responded with love and kindness—and sometimes with pointed comments and questions. Paul asked, "Dad, when we used to go on family trips, why did you always get in arguments with Mom about directions and map-reading, and then get angry with her? You always acted like you had a great sense of direction and never paid much attention to maps. And you never wanted to ask anyone for directions."

This was hard for Jack to hear from his only son, but he owned up and said, "Paul, it was sin and stupidity on my part. It was just pride. Will you forgive me for it all?" Paul did, with a very gracious spirit.

We also mentioned to our children the sins from our family heritages that had plagued our own relationship. We asked God to release all of us from guilt, and especially from a spirit of pride and condemnation. I felt clean before God and at peace—satisfied that I had done something consciously to please God. Yet there was no sense of doing my duty in a mechanical or moralistic manner. I simply wanted to see God honored in our family and in the future generations.

Interestingly, one immediate benefit of all this was better health for me. In Ireland my health began to improve after Jack prayed for me. But now my energy level was raised higher. My sinus allergy problems seemed to have disappeared, and I moved and walked as if I were at least ten years younger. Unbeknownst to me, Barbara began to notice these changes. She later told me, "I had told myself that people really don't change, especially older people. Yet here I could see you and Dad changing before my eyes. It was reaching my conscience."

Grace Glimpses

The root sins of the generations will be handed on if they are not consciously renounced and forgiven.

- You may think that once you have taken a stand against a codependent relationship, you are entitled to "normal" relationships. But this is rarely what happens. The fallout from the previous generations' sins (or those of your own generation) continue, perhaps in a disguised and different form. (In my case, my mother's alienating spirit resurfaced in my relationship with my husband, in spite of my assertions of independence from her paranoia.)

- This iron law of the past can only be overcome by forgiveness that is based upon a deeper knowledge of God's forgiving love revealed in the message of the cross.

Prayer: Lord, grant me a heart to forgive my parents. Teach me how to bless them. Please show me how I continue to be like them even if I don't do what they do. Thank you for your comprehensive forgiving love for me. May I forgive and love my parents in this same way. Amen.

---

1. Catherine Marshall, *Something More* (New York: McGraw-Hill, 1974).

9

Stepping into Partnership: Confident As God's Child

To make sense and feeling the judges of our spiritual conditions, what is it but to make ourselves happy and miserable, righteous and unrighteous, saved and damned in one day. . . . Be much in believing, and make only the Scripture the judge of your condition. . . . If you resolve to make sense and feeling the judge of your conditions, you must resolve to live in fears, and lie down in tears.
—Thomas Brooks, *the Golden Treasury of Puritan Quotations*

Jack, how could you do this?" I held a letter in my hand from a pastor in Florida. I waved it at my husband as he came in from the carriage house now turned into a study.

"Do what?" he asked, looking puzzled. He was in for his morning coffee break, and still absorbed in his writing.

He had accepted an invitation to speak in a church in Florida, and he had told the pastor (without consulting me), "Rose Marie, I'm sure, will want to come along with me. She can teach the women while I teach and preach to the men."

"Why did you make this decision without talking to me about it?" I exclaimed. The pastor of the Florida congregation had written, "We are looking forward to your coming, and we are pleased that you are bringing your wife to teach the women."

"God has done great things for you," my husband said, as I slowly calmed down. "Surely you'll want to pass it on to others." He added confidently. "You can teach on hospitality and on how women can be godly influences by opening their homes to the needy. You are good at this. Since you have started taking in younger children, God has used you even more than when we took in the young adults. Look, you know what works and what doesn't. Just talk about what you know."

Jack was referring to our taking in foster children from various agencies beginning in early 1977. This had been done under my leadership and with his support. Nonetheless I groaned, "I don't know how to talk about it. I can't talk about hospitality; I'll just make them all feel guilty. I know how guilty I feel when you tell me to do something that I don't know how to do—or don't want to do. I don't want to make hospitality a new law."

This was a valid point, but other lessons were at work. Jack had a lot to learn about me, and so did I.

Out of the Comfort Zone

The orphan mindset still dominated my thinking, especially when it came to moving out of my comfort zone. I also did not see the connection between a heart submissive to God and the workings of grace. At this point I did not want to teach women I did not know in a strange church setting. Family, old friends, needy children, and my house—that was my ministry horizon; that was where I felt secure.

But Jack was correct about the need to use what God has imparted to you. Lessons not used tend to lose their power in your life. And this is exactly what had been happening to me. As the memory of God's working was crowded out by work and busyness, I had lost some of the confidence and freedom I'd gained the previous year. In fact, my spiritual confidence had now eroded to the point where fears could move into the vacuum.

My heart cried out, *Please, Lord, let me stay home.* Fears talked loudly to me, and I listened. Therefore, I had little room for loving the women in the Florida church. These anxieties were accompanied by shadows of guilt, which always returned when I fell into self-centeredness. The frightened victim inside me was speaking loud and clear.

Allied to my fears was an excellent defensive game I was playing. Here is how it worked. Fear has a blinding power. I was afraid to speak in public, but I told myself that Jack was dominating me once again, trying to get me to do his will. I did not ask, *Is it God's will for me to speak in this church?* Instead, I retreated once again, persuading myself that Jack's decision was the issue.

Don't underestimate the power of fear to blind and confuse a life. *Fear is deceptive. It will lead you to fight false battles to protect you from facing the real ones.* My fear of public ministry was so great that no one could have convinced me there was any insincerity in my thoughts and words.

Jack was correct about the need to use what God has imparted to you. Lessons not used tend to lose their power in your life.

Jack tried to ease my fear by suggesting that Suzanne Kepler come along as a partner for me in Florida. Suzanne was a gifted campus evangelist working with our church. Comforted somewhat by the thought of her company, I relaxed a bit.

Probably Jack should have challenged my fears, but at this point I'm not sure that would have helped. And gradually, the habit of many years of doing what Jack wanted took over. In early April 1977, I made plans to go with him.

I listened to Jack for the wrong reasons, but he did have a right to question my fearful attitude. God *had* powerfully taught me in Switzerland about his righteousness, and more recently about forgiveness. Why then was it so difficult to share these truths?

What neither Jack nor I saw was the degree to which I thought like an orphan, especially under pressure. Self-trust and independence were still strong persuaders in my life. My

real problem, however, was that I was not walking in the light
of God's love for me or being led by his love for the women I
was to teach. I did not know that I could start each day claiming
the righteousness of Christ as the only ground for acceptance,
and "relax in the quality of trust that will produce increasing
sanctification as faith is active in love and gratitude."[1]

Certainly I grasped something of the meaning of free justification and adoption by faith, but I had so many fears and
insecurities that my capacity for appropriating Christ's grace
and power in daily affairs was limited. I was not yet able to
use my standing as God's daughter consistently as the power
base for living in close partnership with God and with my
husband. At least not in situations where I might be shamed
by a public failure!

So I agreed to go with him—against my better judgment.
Our daughter Keren drove Jack, Suzanne, and me to the air-
port for the two-hour flight from Philadelphia to southern
Florida.

Everyone in the church was warm and welcoming. But I felt
isolated and spent the first day comparing myself to Suzanne
and Jack. I felt squashed and overwhelmed between
Suzanne's gift of evangelism, Jack's enthusiastic preaching,
and my own fears.

Happily for me, the church graciously put us up in a motel
with a swimming pool. Soon I was in the water, doing laps.
"Swimming," I said, "is what I enjoy." Here I felt at home. But
God's grace stirred in my heart unexpectedly as I sat by the
pool in the warm afternoon sun. Under a clear blue sky, thinking about all my inadequacies, I said to God, "I can't do this
ministry, but if this is what you want me to do, I'll do it. But
please show me how." The surrender was with a characteristic
sigh. When I don't know how to communicate my inner feelings or I am simply overwhelmed, I sigh. My daughters call it
the "Miller sigh." They insist they learned it from me.

I do not mean that this prayer turned me into an instant
success. But it did something better: It helped me to conceive
of the possibility that God could work *through* me as well as *in*
me. That may not sound like much, but it is a big forward

move for a person who is convinced that she does not have even the slenderest hope of change.

I needed that slender hope. After two mornings of teaching the women, I just gave up and asked Suzanne to teach the third lesson. Then I asked Jack to take over, which he did.

I hated to fail, and fail I did. My sole success for the week was that among the three of us, I was the only one who came home with a tan. But a strange thing happened. This defeat did not snuff out the small flame of hope burning in me.

On the flight home, with my face pressed against the airplane window, the tears flowed, and between sniffing and sighing, I wondered, *Why do I have such a hard time trusting God whenever the way before me is unfamiliar?*

Jack is strong on partnership—I had been too. We were partners together in the bringing up of our children, partners in taking people into our home, and now he wanted a partnership of teaching in other churches. New Life Church was growing rapidly, and as it became better known, pastors wrote and wanted help for their congregations.

On the one side, I loved my idea of order, which centered on staying at home, where all was secure or seemed so to me. On the other side, I like to please people, especially Jack. So here I was, squeezed between two idols: pleasing Jack (which spelled risk) and pleasing myself (which meant staying home, where it was safe). The second idol was more powerful. I asked myself, *Why can't I stay home and do my ministry where I feel comfortable?* I could have added, *and in control.*

Not long after our trip to Florida, Jack said to me, "Rose Marie, you like your life to be like a canal that goes straight to the sea. You like to know where you started from and where the end is. But life isn't that way. We are out on the river with all its beautiful vistas, but the river keeps changing its course. There are hidden snags, rapids, unexpected turns, and storms, and sometimes the boat seems ready to overturn. But you have to remember that you are not alone in the boat."

He was right. My problem was much like that of the early disciples during the storm on the Sea of Galilee (Luke 8:22-25). Like them, I knew the Lord was in the boat with me, but I felt he was sleeping. Was he powerful enough to deliver me from the storm? I was to find out.

Learning to Trust

A second trip had been scheduled for Jack and me that month. Before we left, I knew I had to make some kind of preparation, so I planned to teach on the women of the Bible—I felt safe on that ground. However, the New Testament book of Romans kept intruding into my thoughts. Instinctively I turned to it and read it with increasing frequency. I was struck by how many times Paul uses the word *righteousness* in it. I kept rereading Martin Luther's introduction to Galatians about an active and passive righteousness, but still didn't understand its application for teaching in South Carolina, where Jack and I were scheduled to go.

> *I was squeezed between two idols: pleasing Jack (which spelled risk) and pleasing myself (which meant staying home).*

On this trip Clyde and Pat, two young men from our congregation, joined us. Their warm support and believing prayers provided a spiritual power base for the work of teaching. Still, I had no idea that God was going to break into lives. If you had told me beforehand that he was going to do some amazing things through my teaching, I wouldn't have believed it possible.

But there was a quiet moving of the Spirit of grace that first Monday morning in this quiet southern church. After I finished speaking, attractive Joan, the pastor's wife, came to me and asked if I would come home to lunch with her. We were sitting together in her sunny kitchen when she came right to the point. With a clouded face, she said, "I am a very angry person. I am angry at my husband, my children, our church, even the dog. What shall I do?"

With the words of Romans in my mind, I said hesitantly, "I really don't know very much about it. But I think you just submit yourself to God's righteousness and give up trying to build your own record. He will make it all right with you."

She said, "Is that all?"

"As far as I know," I replied somewhat tentatively. "Christ's perfect righteousness and yielding to it is the answer."

Joan got out of her chair, onto her knees, sobbed out all her anger, and said to God, "I accept your righteousness." I was dumbfounded. *What was going on?*

It was such a simple answer to her question, but as she acted on it, she really was changed. She stood up and hugged me with a big smile, tear-filled eyes shining with joy.

The guilty burdens of her life had lifted. She welcomed her husband home that day with joy, apologized to him for her anger and condemnation, and told him, "I accepted Christ's righteousness for my own." Like me, he was astonished.

He said with some bafflement, "But what about repentance? Don't you have to do something more?" She simply replied that she did not know all about that, but she did know that Christ had released her from her load of guilt. She concluded, "And I love you in a new way."

Late that afternoon, I came back to where Clyde, Pat, Jack, and I were staying and told them what happened. They were excited and we spent time together in prayer. We continued to do this each day. I was very thankful for their support. Team ministry does away with the "lone ranger" mentality with its swings from self-glorification to self-condemnation. Then when God works, you can't take the credit because it was a team effort, and behind the team's labor was the working of God's sheer mercy.

The next day, after my second talk, a group of women asked if we could have lunch together so I could tell them what I had told the pastor's wife. Today I was a little bolder. I said simply, "You need a new righteousness; Christ bought it for you. Take it as yours." They said, "Is that all?" Again I said, "Yes, that is all."

At the table with our dessert dishes cleared away we bowed our heads between the coffee cups and asked God for his righteousness. Some of the women were changed right there by Christ. Almost immediately others in the church were influenced by these who were shifting their reliance from their own "good" record to Christ's.

Record building for these women meant living for the approval of family, church, and community. Always trying to look good is a terrible burden to bear. The problem is that your conscience condemns you because you must do everything perfectly. You mentally make a list of how to be the perfect wife, mother, or daughter. If you do fairly well, then you become the judge of those who don't make it according to your lists. If you don't measure up, you either try harder or give up.

To teach every day and then be involved with the women in their problems exhausted me, and by Thursday evening I said to Jack, "I cannot give any more talks this week. Please, will you teach the women Friday and Saturday morning?" This time there was no sense of having failed. In retrospect, I am glad, because his teaching on the law and the gospel gave me a handle by which to explain the truths I had learned.

The next morning Jack spoke about the Ten Commandments, and how the gospel cancels out the demands of the law. He explained it this way: "The gospel enables us to serve God with obedient joy and freedom, because the blood of Jesus cleanses the conscience from the condemnation that living under the law always brings."

This talk helped me to understand more of what Martin Luther was saying about an active and passive righteousness. The active righteousness, if depended on, is often used as a basis for building our own record. The passive righteousness is accepting Christ's record on my behalf.

I knew very little about the work of the Holy Spirit, so I often continued to function with guilt and anxiety. But Jack helped me to see the Spirit's power as he applied the message of the Cross to the lives of these women. Now there was being formed in them a new humility and love for their husbands, along with a deep sense of peace. I was amazed at how quickly Christ helped them forgive and accept their husbands. Once again, I was surprised by grace.

The last evening of the conference, the pastor and his wife shared how their relationship had been deteriorating. Eyes opened wide when they said that on Monday, right before the meetings began, they had had a fight on their way to pick us up at the airport! There was hardly a dry eye in the auditorium as they told how the change in Joan had been the catalyst for renewing their love. She was enabled by the Holy Spirit to look away from her own frustrations and anger to Christ's perfect righteousness, and that enabled her to love her husband!

People pleasing had become an enormous burden for these women; they were plagued by self-condemnation

What had happened to these southern upper-class women? They were heirs to a tradition that values courtesy, authority, the family, and the church. Their social life was conditioned by an emphasis on outward performance and appearance. *What will people think?* or *How will it look?* summarized a great part of their lives—and their entrapment.

The law of God says, "Be thou perfect," and they were trying to be perfectly moral, perfectly dressed, perfect mothers, and perfect housekeepers. Much of their approval system had little to do with God's actual laws or true Christianity; it had more to do with the standards of society and the dos and don'ts so often identified with the Christian religion.

People pleasing had become an enormous burden for these women, and they had the attitude that *Underneath it all I am a rotten hypocrite.* This self-condemnation left them frustrated and angry with themselves and their husbands, and alienated from fellowship with God.

When I told them about my inability to love others in my home, it struck a sympathetic chord in them. Like me before my experience of grace, they knew they did not have the power to love others. Each of them now discovered for themselves that the caterpillar is helpless before a ring of encroaching fire.

They saw that the end of this awful struggle is a righteousness bought for them by Christ, and they simply believed this righteousness was theirs. When we come to Jesus, we take the sinner's place. We stop trying to be what we are not and admit instead what we are. By faith then, we are justified before God and enter into peace.

These church women were different in so many ways from the non-Christian women in our northeastern part of the U.S. Yet I was surprised how these traditional family women were so much like the women dedicated to their "liberation." Both sorts seemed to me to be entangled in a web of rules. It's just that these women were mentally burdened by the old rules while the women's liberationists are loaded down with the new rules.

Today many women have the double burden of career and managing a family. An oppressive load of guilt can come on the conscience if the deeper needs of the heart are not met by a powerful Christ.

Now I knew that the message of the Cross provided an answer to the deepest needs of women, both those who were like me and those who were not. The conscience oppressed by rules, old or new, could be liberated through the righteousness of God obtained by faith in Christ. Rules tell us what to do, not how to find power to be different!

Someone has said, "Witnessing is simply one poor beggar telling another beggar where to find bread." That had been my unwitting teaching strategy in South Carolina, and God had sealed it with his blessing.

This time there were no tears on the plane trip home. God had changed the "sighing surrender" in Florida to a growing faith in the power of the gospel. I had seen the women in South Carolina change radically under its influence. The marvel is that it also changed me.

The beginning of change comes when we tell God honestly that we can't do something. The next step is to ask him to teach us to do the impossible. God really did above and beyond what I asked or even thought. He changed the women. He permitted me to have a part in this change. He also taught me through Jack's teaching how to keep a good conscience before him.

I did not then understand all the implications of these new discoveries. But one major change took place. I was never again afraid to speak in public.

Partnership with the Father meant a surrender to his will. And grace enabled. Now Jack and I were partners together in a speaking ministry. I was on a new road, a road leading into a deepening experience of Christ's love.

 # Grace Glimpses

Emotional problems, especially fears, are often rooted in ignorance of the spiritual empowerment to be found in our justification and our union with Christ.

- I had the gifts to teach the Bible but could not do so because I tried to do it by relying on my own human powers. Once my faith shifted to Christ and his righteousness, I discovered the message of the gospel could change me and those I taught in amazing ways.

Prayer: Our heavenly Father, grant me the grace to humble my heart in a new and deeper surrender to your will. Teach me to pray from the heart, "Not my will but thine be done." Then grant me the boldness to bring the gospel to a needy world. Amen.

---

1. Richard F. Lovelace, *Dynamics of Spiritual Life* (Downers Grove, Ill.: Inter-Varsity Press, 1979), p. 101.

Part IV

GOD'S FAMILY GROWS

For you did not receive a spirit that makes you a
slave again to fear, but you received the Spirit of
sonship. And by him we cry, "*Abba*, Father."

Romans 8:15

10

Going Further:
Spiritual Warfare

Now have come the salvation and the power and the kingdom of our God, and the authority of his Christ. For the accuser of our brothers, who accuses them before our God day and night, has been hurled down. They overcame him by the blood of the Lamb and by the word of their testimony; . . . Therefore rejoice, you heavens and you who dwell in them!—Revelation 12:10-12

What happens when a deeply suppressed disappointment—and the anger over that disappointment—has been substantially removed from your life?

The first answer is . . .

You wake up to the fact that you have had the wrong enemies, and you are eager to fight your real ones. I was now deeply grieved in a healthy way that I had seen my husband as my opponent and betrayer for entering the pastorate.

The second answer is . . .

You now have a new openness to God and people. For me it meant that my conscience was much more at peace, and I had a new sense of partnership with God and my husband. Now that the fears were gone I looked forward to speaking with Jack in Texas.

Herschel was wearing a big smile when he greeted me at the Houston airport. Herschel was a former seminary student of Jack's, and he had become a zealous pastor, following the development of New Life Church with great interest. He had invited us to speak at a church conference he had organized.

It was to be held in an inner-city church, with Jack, Ron Lutz (Jack's copastor), and me as speakers. Jack was slated to speak first in the San Antonio area, and I had come along to speak for three days to the women—without Jack's shoulder to cry on if things went wrong. Today I did not think about failing. My mind was not really that much on my success or failure but on what I was going to say about Christ. I was to speak several times to the women, telling how grace had so frequently rescued me from a ring of fire. I planned to teach them the truths Jack had presented in South Carolina about justification and the liberation of the conscience.

As we parked near the church in Houston, I looked at the signs of urban blight and thought, *These folks have one tough mission field!* But the setting had not depressed the spirits of these Christians. When we worshiped together that Friday evening, they were filled with praise for Jesus, and so was I.

When I spoke to the large gathering of women, I led out boldly with my theme. "Freedom," I said, "belongs exclusively to those who are sons and daughters in Christ. It's yours through faith in Christ, not through presumption."

Faces brightened with interest as I talked about the difference between faith and presumption and illustrated the difference, using my experience in Switzerland. This time I spoke more about the power of Christ and clearly contrasted faith in him with a crippling self-sufficiency. As I talked about Christ's gift of righteousness received through faith, the women responded well. They accepted my teaching stance as a learner-struggler who must give all the glory to Christ because she messes up so often.

The words "in Christ" lingered in my mind after the meeting. "In Christ," I thought, means . . . well, I wasn't quite sure of the full meaning, though I had used the words several times in my talk. I knew Jack would say, " 'In Christ' means partnership through faith. We are believing partners with the King!" In his view we praise Christ as the Mediator-King. As a result, we build strong faith in the triune God.

Now my own speaking was giving me a bigger view of Christ. The more I talked about him, the more I became convinced of his reliability, love, and power. I thought, *Well, if that's what Jack means by faith and partnership, I like the idea a lot.* I began to understand that I must submit first to God. When that gets straight, then I have the power to follow Jack. When that happens, we are walking together in partnership. I would lose this concept again and again, but it was beginning to take hold.

During the worship, many of the songs honored Jesus as our Mediator in heaven, who sends his Spirit to work with power on earth. At the close of my presentation, the often hesitant Rose Marie boldly pleaded with these women, "Please pray for my daughter Barbara." After the appeal a number of women agreed to pray for her, and did so right then.

Afterwards, just as I went out the door, a kindly Christian woman shook my hand warmly and gave me a tract. I took it and read the title, "How I Learned to Pray for the Lost" (L. M., Back to the Bible).

It was a pamphlet on praying with biblical authority for the unconverted children of believing parents. The idea of praying for Barbara with authority—well, it was a new thought to me. But it was a natural unfolding of what I had already been learning.

As I read, hope for Barbara's renewal stirred more strongly in me; hope that had almost died in 1972, when Barbara and I had clashed. While meditating on this tract, I did not hear any voice, but I knew God was telling me, *Here is something you can do. Come, be a partner with me; I, the sovereign partner and you, the junior partner. Pray not as an isolated individual crying in the night, but as a partner with your heavenly Father. Call upon me; try me. And my Son will defeat the blindness of sin in Barbara's life and free her mind from the dominance of the devil.*

On the third day of the conference, Jack arrived. I welcomed him with enthusiasm. As soon as we could, we slipped out of the meetings to walk through the sunlit streets of Houston. As we walked arm in arm in the pleasant weather, I showed him the tract. We then found a park bench and sat down, and I began reading to him.

I said, "Jack, it's talking about praying with authority for lost children of believing parents. Let's claim the authority of Christ over Barbara's thoughts, and on the basis of the shed blood of Jesus, claim her from the dominion of Satan."

Jack listened intently. His spirit resonated to anything that might help Barbara, and he said, "Keep going."

"Matthew 18:19-20 teaches about praying with authority. It begins with two or three people agreeing on an issue and then praying in Jesus' name. The author says that agreeing together about what we want and basing the prayer on the authority of Jesus' name will bring about the working of God. Let's agree on this and pray together against the sins we see in Barbara."

He looked puzzled. "You mean we haven't been doing that?"

"I don't think so. Not in this clear way as *partners together* when we pray. We often pray for her in a general way, like 'God, save Barbara from her sins,' 'Bring Barbara to Christ,' but we don't pray against specific sins and bondages and in partnership with this promise."

An Introduction to Spiritual Battle

We then identified her besetting sins as deception, lying, excuse-making, and sensualism. Then we worked out the key elements involved in this kind of praying. Here was the order we followed:

Confess unbelief.

We confessed our unbelief; that is, that we had been praying for Barbara with a negative image of her future, without praising God for Christ's power to change her. We confessed that our minds had been clouded with doubts fueled by Satan (James 1:5-8).

Claim the sovereignty of Christ over the lost person.

We asked for grace to shift our eyes from Barbara and her rebellious behavior to Christ as the triumphant intercessor and ruler at the Father's right hand (Heb. 1:3; 7:25; 9:24). Our plea was Christ's ownership over the children of believers—coupled with a definite rejection of Satan's false claim of ownership of the child.

Agree together to pray against specific sins.
We read Matthew 18:19-20, which says, "Again, I tell you that if two of you on earth agree about anything you ask for, it will be done for you by my Father in heaven. For where two or three come together in my name, there am I with them." We agreed to pray as partners against the four specific sins that we had seen in Barbara's life.

Pray against demon influence over these specific sins.
In a spirit of oneness, we then prayed simply and quietly for the Father in heaven to overcome each of these sins and to rebuke each demonic being that was blinding her. We prayed against each sin by name. Each time we also prayed in the name of Christ, claiming her from the enemy's territory.

Give thanks: Praise God for the answers then and there.
We concluded by giving thanks for God's having already answered our partnership prayer. We thanked him for overcoming each sin we had prayed against, and praised him for the defeat of Satan and his evil powers (Mark 11:22-24).

It was quiet, believing praying, resting in the authority of Christ. We asked the Father clearly and specifically to do what we wanted for his glory. We did it within the context of praise of the sovereignty of Christ and in submission to his person and will. We were relying, not on a formula, but on the atoning sacrifice of the Son of God as the basis for our intercession and praise.

Surprising Results
About a month later, Barbara walked in the back door and went up to the third floor, where Jack was recovering from the flu. Her face was less clouded, and she smiled as she said, "Dad, do you think you can handle some good news from me for a change?"

Jack quickly forgot about his illness. "Just try me," he laughed. Sitting relaxed at the foot of the bed, she said, "The strangest thing has been happening to me. You're not going to believe this. You know what a liar I am?"

Jack nodded.

"Well, I'm having trouble lying! It makes me uneasy. And I am no longer comfortable cheating and blaming other people. I've even gone down to the IRS and told them I cheated on my income tax last year!"

Jack almost fell out of bed! Our joy went beyond words. From then on I prayed with a spirit of faith for Barbara, not with a spirit of fear and worry. On a most practical level, I could more clearly see that God was not against me, but for me! The crippling doubts issuing from the powers of darkness were being exposed by the present, working power of the Lord.

We were relying, not on a formula, but on the atoning sacrifice of the Son of God.

Like many parents of erring children, we had been praying a generalized prayer for Barbara's conversion—almost a rote prayer offered repeatedly but with declining hope. Now we were sensing that prayer is partnership with God coming to expression in words; as partners together, we were praying in communion with the King of the universe. We were putting our eyes more on God's authority and less on what Barbara was doing. We were rejecting the sovereignty of Barbara's rebellious attitudes, the sovereignty of Satan, and the sovereignty of all evil over Barbara's life.

The Right Theology

In other words, we were getting our theology straight and finding out what I should have seen all along. Bad theology tones down Christ's sovereignty and often sets in motion an evil emotional chemistry in our inner self. Wrong theology also teaches that you have to contribute a good record to your salvation or you'll never have peace with God. The devil uses that misguided outlook to lead you to think that rejections, disappointments, and failures of all sorts are God's judgment of *you*—your flawed record—and therefore you have no right to pray with confident authority.

As long as I was ignorant of the biblical theology of grace, my mind was the prey of upsetting circumstances, negative feelings, and circles of despair. I had assumed that my problems were primarily emotional and endless. Actually, till now I was too much like Barbara to help her. But having seen that my basic entrapment was spiritual, I knew Satan had used my sinful nature (fleshly unbelief) to persuade my mind that since I did not deserve to see Barbara saved, and because Barbara was so resistant, there could be no mercy for her. At least not for a very long time.

Bad theology tones down Christ's sovereignty and often sets in motion an evil emotional chemistry in us.

Why are so many Christians still mastered emotionally by hesitancies about God, and why do they so often question his willingness and power to save hard cases? And why do so many Christians doubt that he loves them with all the deep caring described in Scripture?

The answer is that *good theology only helps when it controls the inner life.* Today I see more clearly what I only grasped intuitively at that time. Among contemporary Christians, biblical doctrine is often used as a protective shield to keep the inner life away from God's control. I know; I have used it that way. And I have known numerous other people who studied the Bible without any interest in having its teaching change their priorities or bring them into communion with God. They may study the Bible to salve their consciences or to earn brownie points in a spirit of legalistic lawkeeping—not to enter into the life of God.

The Real Enemy

Listen, dear Christian—don't ever forget that without Christ, our inner life is radically self-centered, self-protective, and rebellious. Such a constricted world of self is vulnerable to both Satanic suggestion and condemnation, and is often embittered by unforgiving attitudes toward others. Such an inner life also bristles with self-righteous defensiveness.

But when we submit ourselves to Christ and his will, Christian teaching progressively controls the inner life. And when this happens, biblical truths like *sonship* and *partnership* will interpret and transform the whole person.

When you have fought the real enemy and have rested in God's sovereign control, then you are free to reach out in love.

Another thing happens when we submit to Christ: We learn from him who our real enemies are. This is absolutely necessary before we can battle effectively.

The first "real enemy" in your life is always your own unsubmitted self-life (James 4:1-10). To struggle against your own agendas and passions is at the heart of spiritual warfare. The second "real enemy" is Satan. The one who hates you without compromise is always the power of darkness (Eph. 6:12). Wherever there is self-praising pride, there the devil has much, much influence (James 3:13–4:7).

Why was I so wounded? Because of my mother? My dad's passivity? Jack's sometimes dominance and insensitivity? Barbara's seeming betrayal of us and what we believed?

No, I now saw that the big battle is between Christ and Satan, and that Christ's strategy is to lead us to love and forgive our earthly enemies, and pray for them with the hope that Christ would also transform them into sons and daughters. This form of warfare brings glory to Christ and mental sanity, too, because it fits into reality.

If faith is a primary way that Christ's kingdom power reveals itself in this world, then we are no longer tied up in knots by guilt. Guilt always brings condemnation, but faith in Christ motivates us to pray boldly for the lost. He is not just my Priest-Savior, but he is also my awesome King-Ruler. A big Christ building big faith!

What you know about the power of Christ determines the strength of your faith. Know a little bit about Christ and his omnipotence, and you have weak faith; know more about Christ as sovereign Lord, and you have more faith; know a great deal about Christ, and you are on your way to having great faith (Matt. 8:5-13; 14:22-36).

Over the next months, Jack and I experienced real spiritual warfare as we battled for specific areas in our daughter's life. We learned to recognize answered prayer, and we also learned that prayer must be constant, and that the workings of grace do not eliminate setbacks as the prayed-for person comes to crises and makes his or her own decisions. Here is a rough sketch of our lives during this period.

We began to pray boldly that Barbara would leave her boyfriend, John.

A few weeks later, she decided to leave John; we helped her move home. She got a job as a waitress and enrolled in university classes.

We discovered that she had been seeing John on the sly. Jack and Barbara had a painful confrontation over this. She left to live in her own apartment. This was a blow to us, but I was learning; I didn't fall into despair, as the devil wanted me to. As a family we counterattacked with a strategy of love. Along with Christian friends, we helped her settle into her new living quarters.

More and more I saw the source of this conflict, so when Barbara moved out, I was not discouraged. Any mother can tell you what a breakthrough this new attitude was! My confidence was beginning to shift from what Barbara was doing to what God was going to do. My faith, though, went through some shaky times as I came to know her better.

We discovered that Angelo, the bartender in the restaurant where Barbara worked, had moved into her apartment. By now I had my own sense of partnership with the Father through Christ. Satan's turning up the heat simply drove me to take my shaky self closer to Jesus.

When you have fought the real enemy and have rested in God's sovereign control, then you are free to reach out in love. Angelo was now a welcome guest in our home. At this time Jack asked Barbara and Angelo to read his evangelistic pamphlet "Have you ever wanted a new life?" and give it constructive criticism from a non-Christian's point of view. They responded with useful suggestions about the booklet. His action said to them, "You are my friends, not my enemies." It was also a submitting to them—a showing of respect for their outlook. This humbling of himself led to a new bond of friendship between Jack and the two of them. Jack and I were now drawing them gradually and gently into a partnership with us and with the Father.

# Grace Glimpses

Equipped with God's power, we have the ability like never before to come against evil.

> • As sons and daughters of God, we become partners with him in the great battle for people's lives. Through prayers of faith, we allow God to accomplish works of grace in the lives of others.

Prayer: Heavenly Father, teach me to see that my real enemy is not the person who has abused me, but Satan, the great abuser. Help me to fight the devil, not people. In Jesus' name. Amen.

11

Growing in Ministry: Uganda

There is a tremendous relief in knowing that His love to me is utterly realistic, based at every point on prior knowledge of the worst about me, so that no discovery now can disillusion Him about me, in the way I am so often disillusioned about myself, and quench His determination to bless me.—J. I. Packer, *Knowing God*

As the years unfolded, many men and women would be helped in a fundamental way in their relationship to Christ by the truths of the gospel I increasingly wanted to share. My heavenly Father's strategy in forming me as a teacher was to create the beggar who needed to find bread. I knew he wanted me to teach, not as the well-trained, the competent, and the successful, but as the one who instinctively fled from him and from others, the one who was hurt and broken and yet who was constantly loved and sought by his surprising grace.

It has been, then, the Spirit's work to draw people into my life to taste and see for themselves the goodness of the Lord to the undeserving.

The heart of my teaching has been to bring people into communion with God through presenting the gospel to them. The essence of that communion is the work of the Spirit. He reveals God's love to the soul; that love breaks the power of self-righteousness and the pervasive egoism that yearns for a successful life that others might be drawn to us rather than to Christ.

There were still struggles to overcome. After so many years of being self-centered and self-sufficient, Satan had numerous time-tested tricks to lure me back into an orphan mindset. How was I deceived by Satan, and what lies did I believe? Here are a few:

- "God doesn't understand."
- "You don't have to do what he says."
- "God has withheld something from you."
- "You have needs that he has not met."
- "You can't believe his promise."
- "If it is the right thing to do, you should not have such a big struggle in doing it."

Again and again, God brought me to deal with these false-hoods, and renounce my orphanhood. Satan has not changed his strategies. *His approach is always to insinuate that God is not good and that he is not for us.*

These lies must be resisted. To choose to follow your own will rather than God's is a terrible freedom which is really slavery to your own desires. We are all filled with longings and passions, some good, some bad. But apart from God, these desires lead into unlimited disappointments. As an example of this disappointment, I cite my own desire to live protected within an undisturbed family circle. You have your own agenda, issuing from your wants. Well, just remember: You cannot do what only God can do—control your whole life and provide a reason for living which provides contentment.

A New Direction

One summer day in 1979, the mail brought a letter with an overseas stamp on it. As Jack read it, a look of dismay crept over his face. He handed it to me, and I scanned the page. I read, "Dr. Miller, we ask you to come to Uganda to begin a church like New Life here in Kampala."

We sat down out on our back porch to think about it. Jack said, "This is the first time I have been asked to go some place to minister that I did not want to go. I think there is only one thing to do. I'll ask the elders their advice."

To his surprise, they thought he should go. Our congregation and its leaders had a heart for this stricken country in East Africa that suffered under Idi Amin's dictatorship. Since 1974, refugees had lived in our house and had come to our congregation from Uganda to be cared for by us, and an exiled Ugandan pastor had served as an elder among us. He had since returned to his homeland and was the author of the letter of invitation.

Due to the coup that ousted Idi Amin at this time, we were called frequently from Kampala, Uganda's capital city. Each time the report was, "It's too dangerous for you to come." Finally in October the word came: "Come in November; the country seems safer now."

I was only too happy to continue my life as it was. We were still taking in foster children, and our grandchildren were always in and out of our house, bringing lots of joy to me. What influenced me to say a hesitant yes to the proposal was a retreat the church had that October with David Bryant, a missions specialist. He said that the New Life outreach to substance abusers, rebels, single parents, deaf people, the mentally disabled, and emotionally disturbed persons, must go overseas. It seemed that the timing of his exhortation was from the Lord and directed to me, though it did not help resolve my deeper fears.

Jack had about two weeks of intense struggle over the trip. He often wept. He was considering seriously the possibility that he might die in Uganda, and that it would happen sooner rather than later. He did not seem to be as afraid of post-Amin violence as he was of microbes. Every time he had gone to Mexico, he had suffered from attacks of diarrhea. He expected Uganda to be a repeat—at best.

He also hated to say what might be a last good-bye to New Life Church and our children and grandchildren. But once he had surrendered his life to God's will, his fears disappeared, and I don't think I ever saw him happier. In his new enthusiasm, he persuaded four young men from our church to join us in Uganda in late December.

And so it was that in late November, I found myself on a KLM 747 over the Atlantic. In Nairobi, Kenya, we exchanged the 747 for a Friendship Fokker operated by Kenya Airways. Once in the air, I thought, *I'll die of a bullet in Uganda. This is the end. I hope it is quick and merciful.* Everything learned about God's grace and sufficiency seemed to have gone out the window; it seemed highly relevant to life in Jenkintown, but highly irrelevant in Africa.

To choose to follow your own will rather than God's is a terrible freedom which is really slavery to your own desires.

We flew over Lake Victoria (as large in size as all of Ireland) and touched down at Entebbe Airport on the Ugandan side of the lake. As the plane taxied slowly across the tarmac toward the main buildings, I looked out the window and saw several stately birds standing along the runway. This was my first glimpse of the famous crested cranes. I pointed them out to Jack.

Together we looked at these birds. They had a wheat-colored, fan-shaped crown. Their bodies were pale gray, mounted on long stiltlike legs. Later I learned they are considered by Ugandans to be birds of peace and well-being.

Once out of the plane, I glanced at the modern-looking airport buildings about three hundred yards away. As we walked toward them, I said to Jack, "What are those holes in the buildings?"

"I think," he said softly, "those are bullet holes. Keep the camera in your purse; you aren't allowed to take pictures."

I stared. This definitely was not Jenkintown. *What a strange, deadly world*, I thought. *Not my home at all.*

But our Ugandan friend, now among the top leaders in the government, was waiting to greet us at the airport. Soon we were being driven at top speed down the road in a dark Mercedes to Kampala. The tropical landscape and the sky were beautiful. I relaxed a bit. I especially liked the feel of the air; it was soft and warm. But the beige-colored houses we passed looked like they had not been painted in many years. Poverty was visible in the villages, with some children wearing little more than rags. Two or three burnt-out tanks from Amin's defeated army adorned the side of the road.

Forty minutes later we came over a hill, and there Kampala loomed before our eyes, a beautiful white city set on seven hills laced with green foliage. I was impressed by its unforgettable loveliness.

A Stranger in a Strange Land

Other senses soon betrayed that image to reveal Kampala's true condition. As we drove into the city, our nostrils were assaulted by the odor of decaying fruit garbage. The mounds were piled everywhere. I felt as if I were going to be sick. The condition of the streets did not help my stomach; as we drove across town, the Mercedes bounced in and out of deep potholes. Between bounces I looked at the buildings. Some were gutted by the recent fighting. Almost all the shops were empty. I looked for one without the windows broken out, and did not see a one! Small groups of grim-faced Tanzanian soldiers in jungle camouflage uniforms patrolled the streets.

Soon we drove onto the grounds of the "only safe place" in Kampala—the heavily guarded fifteen-story Apollo International Hotel. The lobby bustled with Ugandans in dark suits; police and soldiers were everywhere. The Ugandans referred to them as "security." But they definitely increased my insecurity.

Our room on the eighth floor was surprisingly light and airy, with a large, glass sliding door opening onto a balcony that overlooked the parking lot. The bathroom was large and modern, but when I turned on the tap to wash up, no water came out. That was a tough moment. No water symbolized to me this whole weary land where nothing seemed to work.

Very thirsty, I went down to the dining room with Ugandan friends and quenched my thirst with tea. The meal was characterized by a great number of wonderful conversations with Ugandan leaders dropping by to welcome us. Jack and I found ourselves with all kinds of new friends among government officials and members of Parliament. The evening's beef eventually arrived and proved to be the toughest cow on the Ugandan plains. I tried my knife; it did not work. I tried my teeth, but they simply could not handle it. I went to bed, my hunger only partly relieved by crackers and cheese we had brought along.

That night both of us slept well because we were very tired—even though our sleep was several times interrupted by bursts of gunfire, some of it very close. In the morning we awoke to the problem of water—or the lack of it. We had heard that you could at least get water for the toilet by using the fire hose in the corridor. Jack went out into the hallway and looked up and down. A neighbor was pulling the long canvas hose from the end of the hall down to his room. Others also wanted it, and when our turn came, Jack unwound the hose and headed back into our room.

I thought, I'll die of a bullet in Uganda. This is the end.

It was funny to watch him. He put the nozzle into the toilet, and a thin trickle of yellow water dribbled into the toilet bowl. Jack shook the nozzle; nothing more followed. "Is that all?" I asked. I now felt dismal at the prospect of a waterless day. Jack said with a grimace, "That's it."

My fears started to kick in. Then for once I stopped myself, rejected the motions of anxiety inside my mind, and said to Jack, "We'd better pray. I mean pray for water."

We did, and within five minutes the water came into the bathroom with a gush. We had left the tap on in the bathtub and the plug in, and the water was already beginning to fill the tub when I stepped into the bathroom to admire it. After this first experience, we learned to fill the tub with water whenever it was running as a reservoir for the next day. There was never any hot water, but just plain water looks beautiful when you compare it to the trickle of yellow guck coming out of a fire hose. This speedy answer to prayer encouraged me to believe once again that God was with us.

I was really hungry when we got down to the dining room for breakfast. Unfortunately, getting water made us a bit late, and the bananas were all gone. "Well," I said, "I'll take the tea and the bread." But the waiter explained that the bread was also gone. I made do with tea. After "breakfast," we decided to walk across town to the Rohanna Sports Club, located on Namirembe Hill. Here was the orphanage and the meeting place for the new church.

We were very conspicuous as almost the only white people walking the streets. Within the space of three or four blocks, we were approached several times by young Ugandans asking for air fare so they could study in the U.S. They were very determined and only gave up when we said flatly and loudly, "No, no, we have no money for air fares!"

Then we took the wrong road and ended up in "bat valley." I was the first one to see "them." There, on both sides of Kampala Road, were tall eucalyptus trees, and hanging from the tree limbs were hundreds upon hundreds of large bats.

I panicked. A looted city, no food, no sure water supply, gunfire at night, now the bats! I began to cry.

Jack comforted me as best he could, and we finally retraced our steps and ended up at the orphanage. After a warm welcome, followed by morning tea and bananas, I was shown by the Ugandan church leaders into a large room where women were making mats and baskets out of straw. I did not know exactly what I was to do or what was expected of me. None of them spoke English, so we could not understand one another.

The women smiled, talked to me in Luganda (the language of their tribe) and tried to teach me the "simple art" of basket weaving, using eight strands of material. I had ten thumbs, and the strands simply refused to come under control.

While Jack trained the church leaders (who all spoke English) I did my best not to make a complete fool out of myself with the women.

I was a stranger in a strange land.

Finding "Home" Again

About three days a week, Jack went with the leaders of the new church into Owino Market, right where it joins Kisenyi slum. I did not know it, but this was one of the most dangerous places in Kampala. Here in this crossroad area, thieves and murderers plotted their crimes each day. Many teenage orphans called *bayaye* also lived there and supported themselves by buying, selling, and thieving. Out here as well as throughout Kampala, everyone was "chasing money"; sometimes they called it "eating money." But whatever the term, out here people were prepared to kill for it.

Jack preached to them and taught them the Bible. Soon I was joining in, speaking about Christ, giving my testimony. I put my arms around them and told them about Jesus. Many of the orphans became Christians. Soon we were having Bible studies that included them right along with the church members.

The criminals, too, showed an interest in the gospel. Our Christian friends would approach this place of stalls, burning mounds of garbage, and groups of men plotting crimes, and sing "Jesus Is Passing By." Before long, whenever they saw us coming, they would begin to sing, "Jesus Is Passing By."

In the hotel the food was getting worse, and Jack was often terribly sick with dysentery. Finally we went to a doctor, who told him to be very careful about eating the hotel food.

I was slowly beginning to adjust to living in Uganda. But one thing I did not want to do was go to the big outdoor market and buy food. About ten feet of decaying fruit was piled up in one corner, and I imagined a dead body buried underneath it all, and rats making it their home. I didn't know the prices of the food, and I couldn't communicate with the people. I was paralyzed by fear. And fear is always irrational. But we had to do something. Both of us had lost substantial weight and were getting weaker.

One afternoon Jack and I were walking back from Rohanna on our way to the hotel. When we drew near the Nakasera Market, he smiled and, without telling me what he had in mind, took me by the arm and walked me in the direction of the market.

I was simply terrified. I tried to think of something to say— anything. I was looking for a good excuse for not going in there. He took advantage of my silence to lead me, gently but firmly, from stall to stall. Soon he was laughing and joking with the sellers of fruits and vegetables.

I relaxed a little. Jack made purchases, and soon my bargaining instincts took over. I picked out a fresh pineapple and paid for it. Later in our room, we sliced it up and devoured it. Sitting there on our balcony, I again wondered, *Why was I so afraid?*

I had no immediate answer to that question, but going to the market did solve our most pressing problem. Once Jack stayed away from the hotel food and drank only purified water, his health recovered. The poor quality of food in the hotel, the lack of water, and frequent illness opened up Indians, Muslims, and Ugandans to us. Many came to us for prayer. We now received invitations to eat with them in their rooms, sharing our food.

Finding Grace in the Depths

But the problems we saw in Uganda continued to worsen. It was perplexing. I thought about this fundamentally wealthy country, rich in its soil and climate, rich in minerals, and rich in talented, dignified people, but dominated by exploiters. Amin, the former president, was gone, but the murdering and the robbing were not. The shooting at night was getting worse. Someone told us that every morning the authorities picked up between twenty and thirty bodies left on the streets.

We constantly heard personal reports, or read in the *Uganda Times*, about past and present cruelties. About that time I copied out of the paper this account by a young husband whose wife and two small children had been recently murdered. He wrote in their memory:

> In my absence, at the hands of ruthless,
> greedy, barbaric and merciless thugs, you suffered a humiliating death when they shot you
> at our home.

Memorials like this were deadly, daily reading. They filled my heart with grief and indignation. I hated the pervasive evil that had swept this land for ten years and now refused to go away. Amin had fled the country a few months before, but his brutal exploitation had become a way of life, expressing itself in countless cruelties.

Just one example involved a neighbor at the hotel. Early one morning in late December, Zephar, a Pakistani bank official, suffered a severe heart attack in his hotel room. Jack went to the hospital with Zephar and prayed for his healing. He recovered so rapidly he was soon back "home" in the hotel. All the Asian Muslims were deeply impressed by this answer to our prayers.

But a day or two later we found hotel employees moving Zephar's family's furniture out into the hallway! They had walked into the room and, without warning, began carrying chairs and rugs out the door. Safuda, Zephar's wife, was crying and arguing with them. Zephar was very upset, but the hotel employees were treating them with contemptuous indifference.

Immediately we insisted they stop. Jack's anger seemed to bring them to their senses, and they stopped the whole wicked business. It seems that the bank where Zephar worked had neglected to pay his hotel bill, and now he and his family were being evicted, without warning of any kind by the government authorities operating the hotel. Bitter treatment for a man just recovering from a heart attack! We prayed and then went to friends in the government, who straightened out the mess.

Just as I was finding the rough-and-tumble Ugandan life overwhelming, the Father intervened. Bishop Kauma of the Church of Uganda (Episcopal) invited us to go with him to a confirmation service in a village about thirty miles outside of Kampala, on the Bomba Road.

The bishop, a gentle and loving Christian, made us feel very welcome as we drove over the rolling green hills, past the roofless homes of Nubian soldiers who had served Amin. The roofs had been pulled off by the Ugandan populace in retaliation for the Nubians' crimes. Children holding flowers lined the driveway up to the church. This was a very special day. The whole village had turned out to welcome the bishop and us, and to worship and celebrate. Before the service we were served tea, slices of liver, and hard-boiled eggs, all with great ceremony and joy.

Jack had been invited to speak. His subject was Doubting Thomas. I sat on one side of the church building, looking out over the green valley, watching the white clouds float across the incredibly blue African sky. *Am I like Thomas?* I wondered. He was full of doubts and questions, and so was I. Both of us had much trouble understanding God's purposes—and, in my case, trouble seeing how anything made sense in the raging evil sweeping this land. I was deeply troubled by my lack of love for people and my inability to cope with all the evil I was exposed to.

I could see that allegiance to self was radical in Uganda—to the point of destroying it. But I did not yet see that my own reaction to the raging self-centeredness was part of that same kingdom of self. Such self-knowledge could only come with a further disclosure of God's grace—which now took place when I took Communion.

When I went to the front of the church building to take the bread and wine, it was as if Christ were there saying, *Rose Marie, I forgive you for your fears, your unbelief, and your lack of love for these people in Uganda. This Communion is the remembrance of my body broken for you; this wine is the remembrance of my blood shed for the forgiveness of sins—your sins and the sins of all here who believe. Take this forgiveness for yourself, and then forgive as you have been forgiven.*

The gospel was applied to my soul, and my heart responded with joy and thanksgiving. Much to Jack's astonishment I later said, "This is such a wonderful country, I could stay here forever." I had come to Communion as a sinner, and Jesus forgave the guilt of my sin. With a renewed heart, I now loved the people.

The shooting at night was getting worse. Every morning the authorities picked up between twenty and thirty bodies.

After the service, the whole village gathered on the green hillside to eat. What a wonderful afternoon with the Ugandan women in their colorful dresses, children laughing and running, and Jack and I eating with the bishops a marvelous array of goat meat, *matoke*, rice, peanut sauce, and cooked greens. We were the only ones using forks.

On the drive back to Kampala, we stopped to visit a poor woman, widowed by Amin's soldiers. She had ten children and almost nothing material except her small house with its dirt floor swept clean and a few small stools. But she was rich in her love for Christ. There was not a hint of bitterness toward Amin or his henchmen. As we talked with her over tea, she explained in a soft, quiet voice, that she had forgiven them and had nothing but love for her enemies.

Before this I had been shocked by the evil in this land, and now I was stunned by Christ's power to create goodness in a human heart. I will never forget this little lady with her faith and joy. As we said good-bye to her and gave her some shillings, I knew she was no orphan in her heart. This woman had an extraordinary dignity in the midst of great poverty and suffering. The difference in her was the childlike simplicity of her faith.

Larger Dimensions of Evil and Love

Here was the issue for me now. I was encountering evil at every turn in Uganda. Until now my forgiveness of others had been real enough, but it had been limited to a very narrow circle—family, fellow church members, and people who lived in our home. Now God wanted me to learn to forgive and love in a much wider sphere. God wanted me to forgive even those people who had not wronged me personally but had wronged other believers or groups of people.

Soon government leaders came to our room in the hotel and asked for prayer on behalf of the government. Dramatic answers followed again and again as we prayed.

In late December the rest of our team arrived at Entebbe, much to my delight. The ministry burden was now shared by a whole team. David, Bob, Walter, and Philip came through customs looking robust and full of faith. Soon we had them all doing different things, but one thing became an unusually powerful ministry—it was the worship and preaching at the edge of Owino Market and Kisenyi slum.

In a sermon delivered in the mud, tall, blond David said to our familiar audience of *bayaye*, thieves, prostitutes, murderers—and a few ordinary people:

"In Uganda everyone has been wronged by someone. Each of you has experienced terrible wrongs. But God is King, and he gives you a choice: Get revenge or forgive your enemy. But if you get revenge on your enemy, he will get revenge on you. Where will it end? The cycle of getting even will go on forever. Forgive your enemy, and you will break the cycle and know God's way for overcoming evil and renewing your nation."

The day after Dave spoke, Bob almost lost his life because a murderer mistakenly assumed that he was a CIA agent hired by the Ugandan police to capture him. But in the encounter Bob preached the gospel to him and the man was converted.

From "John" I learned a great deal about what went on in the minds of the exploiters, abusers, and murderers around

me—and about human nature. The young man had been lust-
ful, violent, but also suspicious and incredibly self-righteous.
He felt like a victim, and was caught up in self-pity, blaming
everyone but himself for his behavior. Recently he had killed
two policemen "to get even" and, until he heard the gospel,
had felt completely justified in his actions.

As John talked, I could see how much his previous thinking
was like mine—filled with a sense of our own moral superiority. As I heard his story, I saw that self-righteousness is
profoundly evil, and that it makes it impossible to forgive
others completely and from the heart, as Jesus commands in
the Gospels.

It keeps us from seeing our own sins (like pride and hypocrisy) because we have avoided more notorious ones (Rom. 2).
This sense of our own perfection then prevents us from forgiving others because they have offended us in our righteous
superiority. It justifies our judging, condemning, and gossiping about them (Luke 7:36-50, 18:9-14; Matt. 23; Gal. 5:15).

But how did this new perception help me? Well, let me tell
you how the self-righteous person really feels on the inside. I
am talking about myself. He or she gets satisfaction from putting the label "evil" on other people and their actions, but he
or she never puts the label "evil" on his or her own self-
righteousness. So the inner life is characterized by intense
self-deception. He or she says, *I am a victim; other people have
wronged me. I don't deserve this. I am entitled to feel sorry for
myself and blame others. None of it is my fault.*

I found the basis for an important change in my life by
saying, timidly and hesitantly, of my self-righteous, victim
stance: *This is evil; this is the flesh, not the Spirit. It is part of a
raging kingdom of evil, and it leads to murderous anger, if not to
murder itself.*

I had admitted, somewhat reluctantly, that there was a
Uganda in my heart. I had to take responsibility for it before
God. My blame shifting was morally ugly, as ugly in me as it
was in the hotel manager who told his staff to evict Zephar's
family or in the thugs who would murder a man's wife and
children. This healing confession was a gift of the Holy Spirit,

who brings us into partnership with God by calling us to walk in the light.

Grace Glimpses

God brings us into new situations to strengthen our faith and give new dimensions to ministry.

- Sometimes we experience discomfort, as God brings us to a new "place." However, if we continue to walk in the faith of confident sons and daughters, we will see new avenues and manifestations of God's grace and saving love.

- As we see evil in its many forms, it teaches us more about the evil in ourselves. And what we already know about our personal sins can help us better understand evil in larger contexts.

Prayer: Thank you for the power of the blood of Jesus to forgive my sins and the sins of other people and groups. Help me to love what you love and hate what you hate. Help me to apply forgiveness, not only to individuals who have hurt me personally, but to the many groups who have hurt others—even whole societies and nations—by their evil. Show me how to make forgiveness real to these people so that they can be free of Satan's schemes. Amen.

12

Submitting to Sovereign Love: An Orphan No Longer

We should make a deliberate effort at the outset of every day to recognize the person of the Holy Spirit to move into the light concerning His Presence in our consciousness, and to open up our minds and to share all our thoughts and plans as we gaze by faith into the face of God. . . . We should look to him as teacher, guide, sanctifier, giver of assurance concerning our sonship and standing before God.—Richard F. Lovelace, *Dynamics of Spiritual Life*

The evening light was rapidly fading as we drove up to the Nairobi train station. In a few moments we had located the train soon to depart for Mombasa. The train had about it the aura of *Out of Africa* and the days of the British Empire. And we were to be its passengers.

Jack and I thanked our missionary friends, Sandy and Grace Campbell, for making all our travel arrangements and driving us to the station. We waved a happy good-bye. We were on our way to Mombasa on the night train from Nairobi, having flown in from Entebbe a couple of days before. This was our rest and relaxation time. As we stepped aboard, a gracious steward showed us to our sleeping compartment. It was wonderfully old-fashioned in its polished woodwork and firm beds, a holdover from a bygone age.

When we went to dinner, the mood of the dining car was eminently Victorian. Each table had its own small lamp with a fringed shade. There was just enough light to enable us to see our food and each other. The inexpensive dinner was delicious, ample, and served with style. It was fun eating together by ourselves without pressure. We talked and talked, right through dessert and coffee, like two kids on a holiday. We reviewed all the events of our time in Uganda, and decided that we had lived a lifetime in a few months.

In the morning we were awakened by a bell and the porter bringing tea. After stretching myself awake, I opened the wooden window shade and saw staring at me, close to the train, a very tall giraffe. What a great way to begin my vacation! It felt good to be in this ancient port on the Indian Ocean. Here I could relax, swim in the ocean, and be refreshed. But once again, Jack and I turned out to have different agendas.

When we stepped off the train, into the sultry atmosphere of Mombasa, we were met by missionary friends of Sandy and Grace. They drove us to our guest house near the beach district. On the way they invited us to join them that evening in witnessing to the Asian Muslims who gathered in a park overlooking the ship channel. Jack was ready to go, and since I did not want to stay by myself, I said I would come, too.

An hour before sunset, we were taken to the park, where many Muslim families were visiting, laughing, and munching on *pili-pili*—hot, spicy chips. Soon one of the missionaries handed Jack the microphone and asked him to preach. He agreed somewhat reluctantly. Many of the Muslims were pretty far away, and not one of them was even looking in his direction. It was like preaching without an audience—and that is one thing he does not like to do. He felt he needed to get their attention but did not know how.

In the meantime I had found a bench at the edge of the cliff overlooking the blue-green channel. I was watching with fascination a stately ship sailing into the harbor. The air was pleasant, freshened by a slight breeze. I was miles away from what was going on behind me. But suddenly I heard over the loudspeaker, "My wife, Rose Marie, will now talk to you about a Christian marriage—how Christ's love helps us to live together."

I was stunned. I hate surprises of this kind. But out of duty I walked over to the microphone and said a few sentences. Now everything was spoiled for me. In my usual "orphan" pattern, I stuffed down my anger. On some levels Jack and I were communicating well, with most of the "walls" down. But it was still difficult for me to tell Jack how I saw things some-times, especially if it had to do with ministry. I always had the idea that if Jack is for it, God must be for it too, and I'd better get aboard—or I would be in big trouble.

Three weeks later we wrapped things up in Uganda, and stopped in Geneva, Switzerland, on our way home. I love mountains, but after a few days, even splendid views of the Alps did not quiet my spirit. I became increasingly restless. The Holy Spirit, my Disturber, was once more on the move. We were to depart for New York the next day. It was cold, but I bought bread, sausage, cheese, and fruit at a nearby store with the intention of having a picnic on the shore of Lake Geneva.

As Jack and I walked along a street near the shore, all the recently suppressed hostility came to the surface. I felt all my restraints giving way. I cried silently; then sobs followed, deep sobbing.

Jack looked dumbfounded, then embarrassed—then very embarrassed. Two or three smartly dressed women walked by, high heels clicking. I paid no attention to them. There, in the middle of the sidewalk, I blurted out, "Why couldn't I cope? Why was Uganda so hard? Why did I collapse so often? Why was I so angry with you in Mombasa? Why didn't I want to speak?"

He said very quietly, "Rose Marie, *you act like an orphan*. You often live as though the Holy Spirit never came, could never help you live in impossible places, and do impossible things. You act as though there were no Father who loves you."

The Holy Spirit took these unforgettable words and pressed them into my heart. I thought, *He is right; that is exactly how I am.* To Jack's complete amazement I stopped crying and handed back his handkerchief. In my heart I prayed, *Lord, Jack is right, I do act like an orphan; please, please help me and teach me to act like a daughter.*

In the next few months I was impressed and encouraged by the way God continued to answer my heart's desire not to think and act like an orphan, but to rely on the Spirit of the Father like a trusting child. Life became much simpler, and my positive influence on others increased.

I always had the idea that if Jack is for it, God must be for it too, and I'd better get aboard—or I would be in big trouble.

The change in me was perhaps most evident in my relationship with Barbara. When Jack and I returned home, we telephoned her in California, where she had gone to work on her doctorate at Stanford University. Angelo and she had married, and we wanted to congratulate them. Jack told them at length what had happened in Uganda. Then it was my turn. The Holy Spirit gave me a freedom and an honesty that had no pretense in it. I told her the details of Jack's and my discussion in Geneva.

When I was through, Barbara said, with tears in her own voice, "Mom, that's the way I am. I act like an orphan, as if there is no God who loves me and cares about me."

At last, the walls were down, and we felt honest love between us. She wasn't calling herself a "feminist socialist" any longer, and I wasn't trying to be the "together Christian." This was truly the working of God's Spirit.

A few weeks later, our daughter-in-law Jill called. "Mom and Dad, call Barbara! She has been trying to reach you. She has become a Christian!" Our hearts and lips sang the praises of Jesus. What a marvelous work of the Holy Spirit to bring two orphans to himself. A month later Angelo, another "orphan," became a Christian. What an exciting time that was.

I now became an observer of the gracious working of God. When Barbara's semester was over, she and Angelo decided to move back home. It was a sweet homecoming. They stayed with us until they settled in their apartment in Philadelphia. Angelo went to seminary and Barbara taught seventh and eighth grade in an inner city Christian school.

Slowly and often painfully, I was learning, as a daughter of God, to trust in the Holy Spirit's counsel. When difficult situations arose, and I felt the heat from that ring of fire, I learned to cry out for help. After all, a daughter doesn't fear her loving father when the bad times come—she turns to him for help! There is no guilt, or retreating, or self-pity. Sometimes in these crises, there was a sin pattern in my life that needed to be shown to me so that I could confess it. Through it all, God moved into my life, lending me a deeper assurance of the Father's love.

A daughter doesn't fear her loving father when the bad times come— she turns to him for help!

The work of the Holy Spirit is to teach us not only to pray and believe like a son or daughter, but also to act like one in the hottest of fires. When we try to go through the fires of trials on our own, we are burned. But the work of the Spirit is to show us our helplessness, and then make a way of escape. Sometimes the way of escape is to do nothing and let him take us out. Other times he puts out the fires. But his work is to always eradicate the self-centered bent of our heart by replacing it with one that wants and delights in the Father's will. This is acting like Jesus.

More Difficult Tests of Faith

In early May of 1980, word came from Uganda that the government of President Godfrey Binaisa had been overthrown by a military junta supported by Tanzania, which wanted to return Milton Obote, Uganda's former president, to power. Many members of the new church had been supporters of Binaisa's coalition government. Now we were afraid that as former President Milton Obote returned from Tanzania, they would suffer persecution. In a matter of days we were on our way to Kampala.

This time I arrived at the Entebbe Airport with a new joy and consciousness of Christ's presence. The bullet holes were still there, and there were a lot more soldiers and military vehicles parked on the tarmac. We were not shunted through customs like VIPs as on our first trip, but were treated like everyone else—and maybe a little worse. In the main building you could feel the mood of suspicion that came with the new government.

In the days and weeks that followed, we were confronted with a harsher Uganda. Hostile soldiers at checkpoints, a darker mood at the hotel, where many of our friends still resided. There were gunshots during the day now. Besides the obvious physical and emotional struggles, Satan waged all-out attacks on our joy.

On my first visit to Uganda I had learned to survive. But now I was ready to make an impact. The Holy Spirit was the author of my joy, and this new quality in my life made me forget myself and gave me a courage that was entirely from him.

As we went to the Owino marketplace one day to preach, we saw armed soldiers everywhere. Someone had shot a soldier here a few days ago, and apparently in retaliation, three Ugandan civilians had been gunned down by soldiers the night before. It had rained and the water had mingled with their blood. The sidewalk and street were glistening in the sunlight with bloody rainwater.

We chose to preach in the large open space between the National Stadium and the market. Things were terribly tense. A group of soldiers wearing jungle camouflage and their officers in their solid green uniforms were trying to grab suspected guerrillas as the people came out of Owino, heading for the bus park.

With our team we attracted a crowd by singing choruses in Luganda. Soon there was a large crowd around Jack, the young men, and me, listening to our witnessing and speaking.

At the entrance to the market, we could see another crowd forming around the soldiers who were searching for guerrilla suspects. This crowd was growing in size, and moving ever closer to the soldiers. We knew that killing could start at any moment if the soldiers panicked. Once they started firing their automatic weapons, they would likely hit us, too. But we also knew that if we stayed there and worshiped, they were less likely to kill the civilians.

The soldiers had rounded up several young men and were putting them into a police vehicle. There was a comic side to it, because the young suspects who were pushed in one door of the vehicle simply walked out the other side. But the crowd around the soldiers increased in size and kept pressing closer. Then the soldiers clicked off their gun safeties. The clicks were followed by terror. With the automatic weapons pointed at the civilians, ready to fire, the whole crowd broke and ran—in our direction.

Soon the first of the human stampede hit our crowd, and these poor people also panicked. The people came at us like a wave of fear, but none of our Ugandan or American Christians moved. The Lord enabled us to stand there, singing and preaching. Had not the angels protected us, some of us would have been trampled. Jack took hold of my arm and held me up so I did not fall under their feet.

Under his suntan Jack had turned white, but he kept on preaching. When he stopped and one of the Ugandans took over the speaking, I said, "Your face is white." He grinned and said, "You'd better believe it. But we can't move, or the soldiers will shoot the people."

The marvel was that I had no fear. I felt the presence of angels around us as we praised God as sovereign over the chaos. The woman who had always needed control was finding joy in trusting God's control over chaos. That day the soldiers did not kill anyone.

Greater Forgiveness

It was during our third stay in Uganda, in 1982, that we lived with our daughter Keren, her husband, Bob, and other workers, in a small house on the outskirts of Kampala. After a disturbing night filled with the roars of bombs and rockets, we discovered that we were living in prime dissident territory. There had been an attempted coup on the Obote government, and it had started in our area. The day that followed was filled with gunshots, screams of men and women, and the sounds of buses loaded with men and boys. Ten thousand men were taken prisoner by the Obote government, many to be beaten and killed.

There is no place for brooding bitterness in the Christian, no matter what the injustice.

In the aftermath, I was walking down Kampala road to the market when the Spirit brought to my remembrance: "It is mine to avenge, I will repay. Do not be overcome by evil, but overcome evil with good" (Rom. 12:19, 21). At that moment I yielded to the providence of God. He gave me the grace to trust his sovereign control concerning the many cruelties I had seen in Uganda: soldiers who killed out of anger, fear, and tribal hatred; thieves who stole and murdered; thoughtless and greedy bureaucrats.

I had learned to rest in God's forgiveness of my sins through trust in Christ, and I had learned to forgive my husband and family. But I had not learned that forgiveness has a comprehensive side. You have to do it completely and constantly. There is no place for brooding bitterness in the Christian, no matter what the injustice.

Since I felt my anger about Uganda's situation was justified, I overlooked a fundamental spiritual reality: Retaining even righteous anger is dangerous to the soul. A righteous indignation has a place for a short time—surely the cruelties and injustices I had witnessed angered the heart of God—but unwittingly I had let my indignation turn into an angry mood.

But God was good. He shone the light of his Holy Spirit into my life to let me know that I had shifted from my secure foundation in Christ. At one point, a good friend led me to see the lack of forgiveness in my life. I got out a sheet of paper and wrote down everything that angered, upset, or annoyed me about people and events in Uganda. I went through the list and forgave everything and everyone I could remember. Going over the list the second time, I asked God to forgive me for my own pride, self-righteousness, and hardness of heart.

I had bowed to God's will and found new strength to take the next difficult step. I asked God to bless all the people on the list. Peter writes, "Do not repay evil with evil or insult with insult, but with blessing, because to this you were called so that you may inherit a blessing" (1 Pet. 3:9). This was the hardest part. I thought, *They don't deserve a blessing. But then, neither do I. However, I need God's blessing, and the promise is, if I will bless, I will be blessed.* The first blessing was the easing of a troubled conscience as I submitted my bitternesses to the only Righteous Judge.

Grace Glimpses

When we admit our orphan spirit to God, then the Spirit moves into the life and simply takes over with power to work in us to truly love others and do the Father's will.

- The nature of the Spirit's ministry is to lead us into total dependence on God and interdependence on one another. His presence brings grace and joy in the most difficult of circumstances.

Prayer: Heavenly Father, thank you for our relationship with you and with each other through the working of the Holy Spirit. Thank you for the grace that enables us to live with self-forgetting joy and courage because we have trusted in your sovereign control over our lives. Amen.

Epilogue

Thou hast kept the best wine till now. . . . So we are no longer bullocks being driven or dragged unwillingly along a distasteful road; but sons, co-operating wholeheartedly with our Father. . . . And so they entered the second drought-consuming experience with "the best wine" held to their lips, and their Master's tender voice saying, "Drink, yea, drink abundantly, O beloved. Even so shall thy leaf be green when the heat cometh." —Isobel Kuhn, Green Leaf in Drought

Albrecht Dürer once paid a visit to Bellini, an Italian Renaissance painter. The great German master was touring Bellini's studio when Bellini said to him, "Before you go, I want you to give me one of those marvelous brushes you use to paint human hair." Dürer reached over and took one of Bellini's own brushes, dipped it in paint, and, with a single movement of his hand, left on a nearby canvas a lock of hair with the individual hairs perfectly defined.

Jack and I were learning that we are ordinary brushes, capable of ruining the canvas of our lives. There is only one reason that we did not ruin our marriage. That reason was found in the Hand that held the brush. Our Father knew how to use fallible, finite, weak, stubborn people like ourselves to produce his own picture with every hair in place.

After Keren and Bob's time in Uganda was completed and they went home, I struggled with an incredible loneliness. It is so easy under pressure to forget that "sin crouches at the door." In my isolation, I again blamed Jack for bringing me to

Uganda. I told him, "I am tired of always being pulled by your agenda. When we get home, I am never coming back!"

On these last trips I had not been pulled by Jack's agenda. However, he decided that the best approach was for him to return alone, on shorter trips. It was on the next short trip that he suffered a major heart attack.

Before making my preparations to go to Uganda to be with Jack during this crisis, a very important issue had to be settled: Was I going as an orphan or a daughter? God graciously encouraged me from Exodus 33:12-14.

Moses had said to God, "You have been telling me, 'Lead these people,' but you have not let me know whom you will send with me. . . . If you are pleased with me, teach me your ways so I may know you." I, too, needed to know that I was not going to Uganda alone. I read on: "My Presence will go with you, and I will give you rest."

The Spirit revealed the Father's love to my heart, and I believed. My heart surrendered in childlike faith. In that moment I knew the presence of God was with me. Now I was ready and eager to go. I was brought near to God by the mystery of grace working in my life. There was no hint of condemnation from him. I was experiencing, by his grace, an active surrender to his will. I knew I could get on the 747 with my heart saying, *Abba, Father.* I was going to Uganda, not as an orphan, but as a daughter.

Later, a friend told me, "Rose Marie, I couldn't believe how calm you were." I was learning what *submission* is in the life of a true son or daughter. From that time on I was willing to go anywhere in the world.

Submission with joy is the presence of the Holy Spirit filling our lives. This is what happened to me. I knew the conditions of the place to which I was returning. Not too much had changed in the country of Uganda. At this point I didn't even know if Jack would live, but I could endure with joy because God was with me. Where the Spirit of God is, there is freedom. Until now, I had submitted—to Jack's agenda, to God's plans—out of duty that marked the orphan "desperate to please in order to be loved" mentality.

Could I trust the Hand that guided my husband's plans and priorities? Could I trust his Hand over the affairs of men and nations? More practically, could I trust him to get me into Uganda now, since I had no visa? Would he keep Jack alive and restore him to a full and vigorous life? These were not questions fueled by unbelief. These were the basis for my prayers, and my heart answered, *Yes, Lord, I believe.*

The strong sense of the presence of my heavenly Father carried me through the long trip, through passport control, and right to Jack's bedside. I embraced him with a sense of relief and joy that he was alive.

Jack had always been a strong person. But now he was the picture of perfect weakness; his face was white, marred by red blotches. His mind sometimes wandered when I talked with him. I found this frightening. Returning to our home in Kampala, I prayed with tears for his recovery.

Resolving not to be overcome by his weakness or my fears, I said to Jack, "Your ministry is not over. No matter how weak you are, you are going to keep on talking about grace, even if you have to do it in bed with a tape recorder."

Knowing that hundreds of people at home were praying, I recruited prayer in Uganda for Jack. Soon his mental wandering disappeared, his echocardiograph readings improved, and his skin color began to return to normal. By the end of the week his room was becoming a center for evangelism and counseling.

During Jack's recovery, I entered more deeply into the heartland of grace when it dawned on me that "the righteousness of God through faith" was a perfect righteousness.

God's flawless righteousness was mine. I understood now why God was at peace with me, even though so often I was not at peace with myself or my circumstances. *Nothing I could do could ever change God's attitude toward me.*

My heart felt the deep music of this truth. I belonged to him. I was alive because of Christ. There had been so many unhealthy struggles in my life—struggles for reputation in trying to produce a perfect family, struggles to submit to Jack, struggles for personal holiness, struggles to keep my head in

Uganda. This was all a part of my desire to produce something more that would somehow give me that place of secure standing with God and people, and fulfill my deepest longings as a person and a woman.

Someone might ask, "But are you saying that God loves us in our sinning?" Of course he does. That's the whole point of the gospel. He does not love our sinning. He hates sin, but God keeps right on loving his sons and daughters. He chastens us, and for a time may withdraw the sense of his presence from us to awaken us to our sinful moods and actions, but he never takes away his grace from us because it is founded on the blood and righteousness of Jesus Christ alone.

I well remember how I once sought the answers to my questions in all the Christian how-to books. The problem was that it was a how-to that helped the person who wrote the book. I didn't realize that God wanted me to imitate people in their faith, not necessarily in the techniques and patterns by which faith came to expression in their lives.

However, what I usually missed in those books was the foundation that is now so precious to me. Today I am working and failing, and often sinning, but all in the growing knowledge that my justification has brought me into a whole new relationship to the Father.

In a way, I write this with fear and trembling. I still struggle with my mood swings. But I have an anchor in my soul. I know that grace is always for sons and daughters who know and admit that they are not self-sufficient. As part of the family of God, I am still hungry for God and his grace, and strangely enough, a beggar needing all that Christ has to give. Grace always surprises me by the wonder of God's infinite compassion, but his infinite compassion means little if I do not have an infinite need.

I have learned under the patient tutelage of the Holy Spirit that I am not a victim of my past, of Jack's decisions, or of circumstances out of my control. I understand that the pressures and stresses of life force me to deal with myself and with God. When I give up blaming Jack for putting pressure on me, then I am free to be honest in my relationship to him. We have both learned, as God humbled our proud hearts before each other, that grace would control our lives. Jack's humbling went in the direction of not dominating me, not making decisions without consulting me, and not always giving advice when I expressed a need. My humbling was learning to listen to him, to respect him, and to submit to him. We could then pray together through the issues, waiting on the Spirit to lead us in wisdom and agreement. I have learned to trust the providence of God operating through my husband's decisions—good, bad, or indifferent. Like Sarah of old, I need not give way to fear (1 Pet. 3:6).

But what happens when we don't have a meeting of minds? This happened to us when we had to consider putting my mother in a nursing home at ninety-nine years of age. Mother had broken her hip and was extremely difficult and irresponsible in her behavior. Jack, recovering from a major illness, was weak emotionally and physically. When he said she needed to go into a nursing home, I waffled. It was a time of tension and stress for both of us and disruptive to our relationship. A complicating factor for me was the fact that most of our children strongly felt that we should keep her at home.

One day I put my head down on the table, sobbing and crying to God, "I don't know what to do!" Very quietly it came to me, *Rose Marie, you do know what to do. It's time to realize that you cannot keep protecting your mother by making life comfortable and safe for her. Jack is your primary concern. Submit to his leadership.* In submission I had a sense of God's presence and peace with Jack.

I began inviting others to join me in this partnership with the Father through the fellowship of the Holy Spirit. My ministry now became one of bringing hope to women. I especially labored in the area of helping them discern between struggling to live for the approval of others, expecting too much of themselves, or simply resting on God's approval. I also encouraged them to ask the Holy Spirit to be their teacher, counselor, and the revealer of Christ to their hearts.

Here I was, the struggler and rebel, the defensive wife and mother, and a good deal of this was fading from my life. It no longer completely shattered me when Jack corrected me. I who had insisted he listen to me was now eager to learn from him about how to have a growing reliance on Christ.

Nineteen eighty-five was a banner year. Jack was strong enough to return to Uganda, and I was eager to be with him. Following that trip, in Jenkintown, I began a series of Bible studies on Galatians at New Life Church with my son Paul and daughter Roseann. I had spent many long hours questioning Jack and listening to him teach the book of Galatians. Since I seemed to shift so easily from Christ's record to my own, I was eager to learn how to avoid this. Understanding the law and the gospel as Paul unfolds the teaching in this book really helped me. Paul and Roseann had also learned much about God's way of grace. I was later astonished that so many people who listened to the tapes were deeply and profoundly helped.

Another exciting event that year happened when Barbara (seven months pregnant), Angelo, and their two-year-old son, A.J., moved into our big house on Walnut Street. What sin and Satan had wanted to destroy in our family, God had restored and rebuilt. Barb and I were no longer alienated orphans, but mother and daughter, sisters and partners together in the grace of God.

How is life in Jenkintown when I am not traveling? Sometimes I need a backhoe to get into the laundry room to get my wash done. Once I asked my sister to clean the bathroom. Since she can't read, and because the can of parmesan cheese looked like a can of Comet cleanser to her, she scrubbed the sink and tub with grated cheese. And I wonder why I am always calling the plumber!

Someone once asked Barbara how it worked living together for nine years. She replied, "If we had to work at it, it wouldn't work." This is indeed a picture of God's grace in all of our lives.

Ten years ago I realized my perfectionism could not bring happiness or holiness to my children. I unreservedly gave my family to God and repented of trying to lead a family out of my own pitiful resources. God impressed upon my heart that he would build my house. And God did. He not only brought each of our children to himself; he brought their children into the kingdom of his love. And he did more. We not only have twenty-four grandchildren; we have a worldwide family. Indeed this was more than I could ask or think. And God receives all the glory.

Do I still need the gospel? All the time! I drift as easily as an autumn leaf on a windy day. How does this happen? God will use his Word to impress on my heart exciting truths. With this comes a new willingness to obey him, but after a while the truths will fade, while life goes on. I am left dry, empty, and barren. My life then fills up with unlimited obligations and duties without joy. What do I do? I ask the Holy Spirit to show me where and how I drifted. Then I repent of the sins he reveals to me. By faith I rely on the Holy Spirit to change my heart to turn the tasks of life again to joy. During this process I ask people to pray. I have a supportive network of children, grandchildren, church members, and friends all over the world who pray for me. I am humbled and deeply grateful.

This caterpillar in her rings of fire knows with growing confidence that deliverance comes only from outside of herself and from above. I can go with boldness to the throne of grace. The Holy Spirit is my resident counselor, and I can truly depend on his power to convict me of sin, teach me, and reveal Christ to this poor needy heart.

Under the leadership of the renewal ministries of World Harvest Mission, I teach with Jack in our "Sonship" course on the characteristics of orphans and sons, using much of the autobiographical material in this book. I especially emphasize that the language of orphans is complaining, gossiping, boasting, defending, and excuse making. The language of sons and daughters is giving God the glory—boasting in the work of Christ, and sharing this good news with others.

When my story began, I saw myself as much more of a victim than a sinner. I saw the gospel as something that is primarily related to becoming a Christian. The power that the gospel has for me now is that I know there is a safe place where I can leave the load of guilt and sin. I can't lose, because I have One who intercedes in heaven for me.

We are sons and daughters, not left alone to fall prey to our flesh, the world, or Satan's devices and seductions. God is the great initiator in teaching us about grace in all the circumstances of our lives. To all who read this book, may I entreat you to open your heart to Jesus, the One who always lives to make intercession for us. Such a One meets our need for cleansing, for holiness, and for forgiveness. Then respond to that love by reaching out in love to those in your family, your neighbors, and to the world.

I end with a favorite quote:

> "It was I who wounded you," said Aslan. "I am the only lion you met in all your journey-ings. . . ."
> "Child," said the Lion, "I am telling you your story, not hers. No one is told any story but their own." (C. S. Lewis, *The Horse and His Boy*)

In some ways, God has been that lion to me. Through my life crises—my wounds—he has brought healing. And at the same time he has revealed to me my "story." It is a story wrapped up in the larger, glorious story of God's love for the world, and the marvelous plot has been written by grace. At each crucial point, my life can go one way or the other, depending on the choice my character makes. The orphan will take a difficult, hopeless path; the daughter will walk the way of grace, freedom, and hope.

God has a story of grace for you, too. As you listen to the Word of God, and allow the Holy Spirit to plant it in your heart, you will hear the story. It is in the hearing that we learn of the love that can cast out our fears. And when we obey that voice of love, we allow God's grace to live and act through us. God's life *in us*—this is true freedom.

Appendix A

Martin Luther's Introduction to His Commentary on Galatians

I have taken in hand, in the name of the Lord, yet once again to expound this epistle of St. Paul to the Galatians; not because I desire to teach new things, or such as ye have not known before, since that, by the grace of Christ, Paul is now thoroughly known unto you, but for that we have to fear lest Satan take from us this doctrine of faith, and bring into the Church again the doctrine of works and men's traditions. Wherefore it is very necessary that this doctrine be kept in continual practice and public exercise, both of hearing and reading.

And although it be never so well known, yet the devil, who rageth continually, seeking to devour us, is not dead. Likewise our flesh and old man is yet alive. Besides this, all kinds of temptations do vex and oppress us on every side; so that this doctrine can never be taught, urged, and repeated enough. If this doctrine be lost, then is also the doctrine of truth, life, and salvation, also lost and gone. If this doctrine flourish, then all good things flourish; religion, the true service of God, the glory of God, the right knowledge of all things which are necessary for a Christian man to know. Because, therefore, we would be occupied, and not idle, we will begin now where we made an end, according to the saying of the song of Sirach: "When a man hath done what he can, he must begin again."

The Argument of the Epistle of St. Paul to the Galatians.
It behoveth us first of all to see what matter St. Paul here treateth of. The argument is this: He goeth about to establish the doctrine of faith, grace, forgiveness of sins, or Christian righteousness, to the end that we may have a perfect knowledge and difference, between Christian righteousness, and all other kinds of righteousness. For there are divers sorts of righteousness. There is a civil or political righteousness, which Kings, princes of this world, magistrates and lawyers deal

withal. There is also a ceremonial righteousness, which the traditions of men do teach. This righteousness parents and schoolmasters may teach without danger, because they do not attribute to it any power to satisfy for sin, to please God, or to deserve grace; but they teach such ceremonies as are only necessary for the correction of manners, and certain customs concerning this life. Besides these, there is another righteousness, called the righteousness of the law, or the ten commandments, which Moses teacheth. This we do also teach, but after the doctrine of faith.

Above all these, there is yet another righteousness; to wit, the righteousness of faith, or Christian righteousness, the which we must diligently discern from the others aforesaid; for they are quite contrary to this righteousness, both because they flow out of the laws of Kings and rulers, the traditions of the pope, and the commandments of God; and also because they consist in our works, and may be wrought by us either by our natural strength, (as the papists term it) or else by the gift of God. For these kinds of righteousness are also the gift of God, like all other good things are, which we do enjoy.

But the most excellent righteousness of faith, which God through Christ, without any works, imputeth to us, is neither political, nor ceremonial, nor the righteousness of God's law, nor consisteth of works, but is clean contrary to these; that is to say, it is a mere passive righteousness, as the others are active. For in the righteousness of faith, we work nothing, we render nothing unto God, but we only receive, and suffer another to work in us, that is to say, God. Therefore it seemeth good unto us to call this righteousness of faith, the passive righteousness. This is a righteousness hidden in a mystery, which the world doth not know, yea, Christians themselves do not thoroughly understand it, and can hardly take hold of it in their temptations. Therefore it must be diligently taught, and continually practiced. And whoso doth not understand or apprehend this righteousness, in afflictions and terrors of conscience, must needs be overthrown. For there is no comfort of conscience so firm and sure, as this passive righteousness is.

For the troubled conscience, in view of God's judgment, hath no remedy against desperation and eternal death, unless it take hold of the forgiveness of sins by grace, freely offered in Christ Jesus, which is this passive faith, or Christian righteousness; which if it can apprehend, then it may be at rest, and can boldly say: I seek not active or working righteousness, for if I had it, I could not trust in it, neither dare I set it against the judgment of God. Then I abandon myself from all active righteousness, both of my own and of God's law, and embrace only that passive righteousness, which is the righteousness of grace, mercy, and forgiveness of sins. Briefly, I rest only upon that righteousness, which is the righteousness of Christ and of the Holy Ghost. The greatest knowledge, and the highest wisdom of Christians is, not to know the law, to be ignorant of works, and of the whole active righteousness, especially when the conscience wrestleth with God. Like as on the contrary, amongst those who are not of God's people, the greatest wisdom is, to know and to urge the law and the active righteousness. But it is a strange thing and unknown to the world, to teach Christians to be ignorant of the law, and to live before God as if there were no law: notwithstanding, except thou be ignorant of the law, and be assuredly persuaded in thine heart, that there is now no law, nor wrath of God, but only grace and mercy for Christ's sake, thou canst not be saved; for by the law cometh the knowledge of sin. Contrariwise, works and the keeping of the law is so strictly required in the world, as if there were no promise, or grace.

Here then is required a wise and faithful disposer of the word of God, who can so moderate the law, that it may be kept within its bounds. He that teacheth that men are justified before God by the observation of the law, passeth the bounds of the law, and confoundeth these two kinds of righteousness, active and passive, and is an ill logician, for he doth not rightly divide. Contrariwise, he that setteth forth the law and works to the old man, and the promise and forgiveness of sins and God's mercy to the new man, divideth the word well. For the flesh, or the old man, must be coupled with the law and works; the spirit, or the new man must be joined with the promise of God and His mercy. Wherefore when I see a man oppressed with the law, terrified with sin, and thirsting for comfort, it is time that I removed out of his sight the law and active righteousness, and that I should set before him, by the gospel, the Christian or passive righteousness, which, excluding Moses and his law, offereth the promise made in Christ, Who came for the afflicted and sinners. Here the man is raised up again, and conceiveth the good hope, neither is he any more under the law, but under grace. How not under the law? According to the new man, to whom the law doth not appertain. For the law hath its bounds unto Christ, as Paul saith: "For Christ is the end of the law" (Rom. 10:4), who being come, Moses ceaseth with his law, circumcision, the sacrifices, the sabbaths, yea, and all the prophets.

This is our divinity, whereby we teach how to put a difference between these two kinds of righteousness, active and passive, to the end that manners and faith, works and grace, policy and religion, should not be confounded, or take the one for the other. Both are necessary; but must be kept within their bounds; Christian righteousness appertaineth to the new man, and the righteousness of the law appertaineth to the old man, which is born of flesh and blood. Upon this old man, as upon an ass, there must be laid a burden that may press him down, and he must not enjoy the freedom of the spirit of grace, except he first put upon him the new man, by faith in Christ (which notwithstanding is not fully done in this life), then may he enjoy the kingdom and inestimable gift of grace.

This I say, to the end that no man should think we reject or forbid good works, as the papists do slander us, neither understanding what themselves say, or what we teach. They know nothing but the righteousness of the law, and yet they will judge of that doctrine which is far above the law, of which it is impossible that the carnal man should be the judge. Therefore they must needs be offended, for they can see no higher than the law. Whatsoever, then, is above the law, is to them a great offence. But we imagine, as it were, two worlds, the one heavenly, the other earthly. In these we place these two kinds of righteousness, being separate the one far from the other. The righteousness of the law is earthly, and hath to do with earthly things. But as the earth bringeth not forth fruit except it be watered first from above; even so by the righteousness of the law, in doing many things we do nothing, and in fulfilling the law we fulfil it not, except first we are made righteous by the Christian righteousness, which appertaineth nothing to the righteousness of the law, or to the earthly and active righteousness. But this righteousness is heavenly, which we have not of ourselves, but receive it from heaven; we work not for it, but by grace it is wrought in us, and is apprehended by faith; whereby we mount up above all laws and all works. So that, like as we have borne the image of the earthly Adam, so we shall bear the image of the heavenly Adam, which is the new man in a new world, where is no law, no sin, no remorse or sting of conscience, no death, but perfect joy, righteousness, grace, peace, salvation and glory.

Why, do we then nothing? Do we work nothing for the obtaining of this righteousness? I answer, Nothing at all. For this is perfect righteousness, to do nothing, to hear nothing, to know nothing of the law, or of works, but to know and believe this only, that Christ is gone to the Father, and is not now seen; that He sitteth in heaven at the right hand of His Father, not as judge, but made unto us of God, wisdom, righteousness, holiness and redemption; briefly, that He is our high priest intreating for us, and reigning over us, and in us, by grace. In this heavenly righteousness sin can have no place, for there is no law; and where no law is, there can be no transgression (Rom. 4:15). Seeing then that sin hath here no place, there can be no anguish of conscience, no fear, no heaviness. Therefore St. John saith (1 John 5:18): "He that is born of God cannot sin."

But if there is any fear, or grief of conscience, it is a token that this righteousness is withdrawn, that grace is hidden, and that Christ is darkened and out of sight. But where Christ is truly seen, there must be full and perfect joy in the Lord, with peace of conscience, which thus thinketh: Although I am a sinner by the law, and under condemnation of the law, yet I despair not, yet I die not, because Christ liveth, who is both my righteousness and my everlasting life. In that righteousness and life I have no sin, no fear, no sting of conscience, no care of death. I am indeed a sinner as touching this present life, and the righteousness thereof, as the Child of Adam. But I have another righteousness and life, above this life, which is Christ and Son of God, who knoweth no sin, no death, but is righteousness and life eternal; by whom this my body, being dead and brought to dust, shall be raised up again, and delivered from the bondage of the law and sin, and shall be sanctified together with the spirit.

So both these continue while we live here. The flesh is accused, exercised with temptations, oppressed with heaviness and sorrow, bruised by its active righteousness of the law; but the spirit reigneth, rejoiceth, and is saved by this passive and Christian righteousness, because it knoweth that it hath a Lord in Heaven, at the right hand of His Father, who hath abolished the law, sin, death, and hath trodden under His feet all evils, led them captive, and triumphed over them in Himself (Col. 2:15).

St. Paul, therefore, in this epistle, goeth about diligently to instruct us, to comfort us, to hold us in the perfect knowledge of this most Christian and excellent righteousness. For if the article of justification be once lost, then is all true Christian doctrine lost. And as many as are in the world that hold not this doctrine are either Jews, Turks, Papists, or Heretics. For between "the righteousness of the law," and Christian righteousness, there is no mean. He that strayeth from this Christian righteousness, must needs fall into the righteousness of the law; that is to say, when he hath lost Christ, he must fall into the confidence of his own works.

Therefore do we so earnestly set forth, and so often repeat the doctrine of "faith," or Christian righteousness, that by this means it may be kept in continual exercise, and may be plainly discerned from the active righteousness of the law. Otherwise we shall never be able to hold the true divinity (for by this only doctrine the Church is built, and in this it consisteth), but by-and-by we shall either become canonists, observers of ceremonies, observers of the law, or papists, and

Christ so darkened, that none in the Church shall be either rightly taught or comforted. Wherefore I do admonish you, especially such as shall become teachers and guiders of consciences, and also every one apart, that ye exercise yourselves continually by study, by reading, by meditation of the word, and by prayer, that in time of temptation ye may be able to instruct and comfort both your own consciences and others, and to bring them from the law to grace, from active and working righteousness, to the passive and received righteousness: and to conclude, "from Moses to Christ."

Let us diligently learn to judge between these two kinds of righteousness, that we may know how far we ought to obey the law. We have said before that the law in a Christian ought not to pass its bounds, but ought to have dominion only over the flesh, which is in subjection to it, and remaineth under it. But if it shall presume to creep into the conscience, and there seek to reign, see thou play the cunning logician, and make the true division. Say thou: "O law, thou wouldest climb up into the kingdom of my conscience, and there reprove it of sin, and take from me the joy of my heart, which I have by faith in Christ, and drive me to desperation that I may be without hope, and utterly perish. Keep within thy bounds, and exercise thy power upon the flesh: for I am baptized, and by the gospel am called to the partaking of righteousness and everlasting life."

When I have Christian righteousness reigning in my heart, I descend from heaven as the rain maketh fruitful the earth; that is to say, I do good works, how and wheresoever occasion arise. If I am a minister of the word, I preach, I comfort the broken-hearted, I administer the sacraments. If I am a householder, I govern my house and family well, and in the fear of God. If I am a servant I do my master's business faithfully. To conclude, whosoever is assuredly persuaded that Christ alone is his righteousness, doth not only cheerfully and gladly work well in his vocation, but also submitteth himself through love to the rulers and to their laws, yea, though they be severe, and, if necessity should require, to all manner of burdens, and to all dangers of the present life, because he knoweth that this is the

will of God, and that this obedience pleaseth Him. Thus far as
concerning the argument of the Epistle, whereof Paul treateth,
taking occasion of false teachers who had darkened this righteousness of faith among the Galatians, against whom he setteth himself in defending and commending his authority and
office.

Taken from *Commentary on Galatians* by Martin Luther, published in 1979 by
Kregel Publications. Translation by Erasmus Middleton, edited by John
Prince Fallowes. A reprint of the 1850 edition published by the Harrison
Trust, London.

Appendix B

Characteristics of an orphan

Life consciously or unconsciously is centered on personal autonomy and moral will power, with grace understood as God's maintaining your own strength—not as his transforming power.

Faith is defined as trying harder to do and be better, with a view to establishing a good record leading to self-justification.

Obedience is related to external, visible duties, with attitudes and deeper motivation virtually ignored.

"What people think" is represented as the real moral standard, based upon visible success and failure.

An *I-am-a-victim* attitude is supported by coping strategies: wall building, blame shifting, gossiping, and defending. All this is accompanied by intense feelings of aloneness, believing that no one understands and that one is trapped by circumstances.

Characteristics of a son or daughter

Increasing assurance of God as Father through knowledge of the doctrine of the Cross

Building a partnership with God, relying on the Spirit for a willing and obedient life

Forgiving instead of judging and condemning, putting off defensiveness, and learning to listen

Relying on the Holy Spirit to use the tongue for praise and not complaint or gossiping

Seeing by faith God's sovereign plan over one's life as wise and good—a plan not to be feared

Learning to pray; recognizing that we have no resources, and claiming the promises of God

Relying on the Holy Spirit in going quickly to Christ with sins, burdens, and needs, seeking daily forgiveness and cleansing.

World Harvest Mission offers audio and video tapes on these related topics:

SONSHIP: The foundational track of World Harvest Mission's training course, this sixteen-tape series focuses on Sonship and seeks to drill the gospel into the core of the believer's life. Audio: $99.00 Video: $199.00

GALATIANS: An eight-lecture series by Rose Marie Miller that leads listeners to repentance and to Christ. Audio: $24.00

FROM GUILT TO GRACE: A twelve-tape series by Rose Marie Miller on Romans 1–8 that encourages the listener to live daily by grace rather than self effort. Audio: $70.00

GRACE PARENTING: Jack and Rose Marie Miller and their daughter Barbara share, in this seven-tape series, their experiences with parenting and focus on how to reach a child's conscience to have a heart for God. Audio: $45.00 Video: $125.00

Available from
World Harvest Mission
Book/Tape Ministry
222 Pennsylvania Avenue
Oreland, PA 19075
215-885-1811
FAX 215-885-4762